Necessity Is A Mother

Toolbox Tales When All Else Fails

MARTA KNOBLOCH
AND KIP PIPER

Photo Credits:
Cover photo by Bidouze Stephane via 123RF.com
Man with wrench photo by Luca Bertolli via 123RF.
com
Man with hedge shears photo by Olaf Speier via
123RF.com
Horny Toad photo by Petei Guth
Ball jar and lids photo by Margaret and Mitchell Mal-
pass
Clipping from *The Kingfisher Times and Free Press*
submitted by Jack L. Musick and Kathleen Musick
Gancer

CONTENTS

THINKING OUTSIDE THE TOOLBOX

ACKNOWLEDGEMENT

The editors would like to thank Denise "Deni" Gainer for assisting in the editing of the *Necessity is a Mother* anthology.

We'd also like to congratulate her for the winning entry in the anthology's subtitle contest: *Toolbox Tales When All Else Fails.*

INTRODUCTION

The inspiration for *Necessity is a Mother: Toolbox Tales When All Else Fails* came our own personal experience. When we called for submissions, we used this anecdote as a example of funny and wacky situations where a tool or tools are needed but not available, and the atypical and ingenious resources used to solve the problem.

"I don't need a toolbox,
I have a manicure kit."

My friend and I arrived at my new home to find two enormous boxes holding the inflatable beds we planned to use that night delivered on my doorstep.

We wrestled the huge packing boxes into the living room. They were heavy duty cardboard wrapped in reinforced tape. My toolbox was arriving with all my household goods in the moving van the next day. What to do?

After riffling through my makeup bag, I came up with a pair of tweezers and my manicure scissors. We took turns sawing away at the tape and stabbing through the packaging for a sweaty hour of non-P.C. language and possible carpel tunnel. At last we demolished them amid shrieks of triumph, high fives and a victory dance around the room. (Curious neighbors peering through the plate glass window probably thought a demonic cult had bought the house.) After this epic struggle, unfolding the beds was a snap and, miracle of miracles, they inflated themselves when plugged into the wall.

We hunkered down on the hearth for a hard earned "Natty Boh."

"I don't need a toolbox, I have a manicure kit," I toasted.

We were surprised and delighted to realize how broad the concept of a "tool" was to the writers who submitted their work to us. While many of the authors used the traditional definition of a tool: "a handheld device that aids in accomplishing a task" (Merriam-Webster online dictionary), many expanded the idea. So we decided to divide the anthology into two parts: "Toolbox Tales" and "Thinking Outside the Toolbox."

It has been a great pleasure to read and select these individualistic and clever stories, short essays, photos and poems. Our thanks to all of the writers who sent us their manuscripts. We believe the reader will take as much pleasure in reliving the experiences of our authors as we did. There can be no doubt that the spirits of George Washington Carver, Thomas Edison and other great inventors still thrive in the 21st century.

Marta Knobloch and Kip Piper, Co-editors

Toolbox Tales

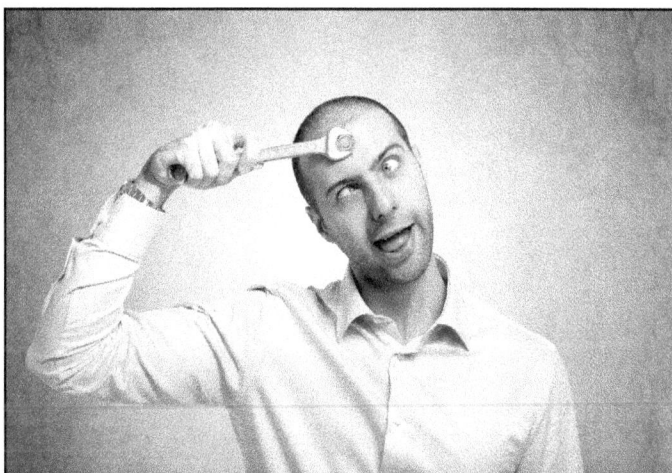

THE SHOW MUST GO ON
Richard Ford

'Twas the night before Christmas, and all through the Community Playhouse creatures were definitely stirring. It was dress rehearsal for our Christmas Day play, written by two members of our illustrious troupe, whose talents, modest though they may have been, were clearly in greater evidence as playwrights than as actors.

All of us appeared to know our lines perfectly, and we had spit and polished our performances to a point that amateurs could take pride in. The coauthors of *Light of Man* were also its co-directors, which had been a source of some friction and frustration along the way, owing to "artistic differences" between the two. Each had attempted to incorporate ("impose," actually) his own interpretive nuances and assert his own particular vision of the production, but in spite of their conflicting viewpoints, we felt that obstacles and impediments had been overcome and consensus reached with a certain serenity. Amid the hectic activity at the playhouse that

Christmas Eve afternoon, there was a stronger sense of confidence and justifiable optimism among the players than we had ever experienced immediately before debuting any of the works in our repertoire.

Our serenity, confidence and optimism were abruptly shaken, however, jeopardized by an unfortunate mishap. In one scene, an angel was to appear (bearing tidings of great joy) and bless the good folks gathered on a remote hillside. The angel's costume was a billowy, white, roby affair, whose folds would be blown about gently and ineffably by puffs of air generated by an off-stage fan. The nuance sought here, as one of the directors explained, was "otherworldliness." There were wings and a halo thrown into the bargain, which might have seemed corny and clumsy, but somehow did not.

The unfortunate mishap occurred when the angel fell from grace. In a moment of distraction, walking hurriedly and tending to his folds, he somehow caused his halo to fall onto the cement floor of the hall leading from his dressing room to the stage. The heavenly prop had been rigged up as a thin plastic ring about eight inches across, fastened with tape and tied with fishing line to a thin, notched bamboo rod that fit into a socket sewn into the collar of the robe at the back of the actor's neck. The plastic must have been quite brittle, because upon impact it shattered into several pieces. The angel was to appear on stage in two minutes.

Poor fellow. Bearing tidings which were now plainly not of great joy, he scurried apologetically to where the directors had been observing the rehearsal, alternately nodding their heads solemnly, knowingly and approvingly. There's been a ghastly accident, the angel must have said, taking his cue from Ray Milland calling the police in *Dial M for Murder*. Rehearsal was suspended for a time to assess the damage.

Woe was us. This show must go on, and it must go on tomorrow, in front of a paying audience. There was sympathy for the disgraced celestial creature, but also exasperation. It was nearly nightfall, and we were all anxious to get home and join our friends and families for a Christmas Eve toast before the hearth.

One of the actors, a shepherdess, had an idea. It was as though a light bulb had illuminated over her head. In one of the dressing rooms, she remembered, there was a fluorescent light fixture fitted with a bulb in the shape of a ring. It was just the right size to be pressed into service in our time of need. The bulb was quickly fetched and mounted securely onto the bamboo stick. The rest of the rehearsal went smoothly, and we managed to leave the theater by about seven o'clock. That shepherdess was our guardian... Well, you know.

The surrogate halo worked like a charm on opening day, a rainy Christmas day, and the play was warmly received. It was even rumored that lightning generated by the storm caused the fluorescent bulb to flicker slightly during the performance, creating a special effect—an otherworldly effect—worthy of the conjurings of even the most spectacular Hollywood moviemakers and Broadway stage wizards

IMPROMPTU RULER
Petei Guth

When my Texas Master Naturalist group took our monthly three-mile walkabout, I found a baby horned lizard. Its body was about the size of a nickel and a little over an inch long. My team members were surprised I even saw it.

We didn't have a measuring tape in our field kit. We did have paper and pens to keep track of our harvester ant hill count.

"Give me a piece of paper and a pen," I said.

I put the lizard on the paper with its tail tip at the edge and then marked the point of its nose on the paper. I could measure the length of the pen mark once I was home.

That little guy was just one and a quarter inches long, but he was the star of the show!

FIXING THE LEAKS
Dana Glossbrenner

My husband, Jim, once worked for our local university as a recruiter. Being cheap, as most public universities are with their lowly servants, the university paid a ridiculous per diem for out-of-town trips. It required conservation on food and gas, as well as lodgings in Motel 6 at best, if an employee on the road expected to break even. But Jim beat them at their own game. He could out-cheap the cheapest miser on the planet when necessity required it.

He carried snacks in a Styrofoam cooler, found local hotels with discounts for the roaches, and curtailed his speed in his already efficient 1976 Toyota Corolla. He drove the car a total of 14 years, logging 216,000 miles on the odometer. He upgraded to a Honda Accord and

9

waved goodbye to the old faithful blue car with no compunction. Not sentimental about material objects, he doesn't hang on to them or mourn their passing. So he gleefully drove away. He didn't feel it necessary to discuss with the car dealer the cat food cans that had become part of the body of the old Corolla. They didn't show.

A couple of years before he finally decided to get a new car, Jim noticed that things in the old Corolla's trunk were getting wet. Since rain is rare in West Texas, he knew for certain that it wasn't rainwater. He washed the car himself at the fifty-cent car wash, and he knew his trunk was empty the last time he aimed the water wand at the car for its bi-weekly bath. And the seal around the trunk was fine. Finally, he lifted the threadbare carpet and discovered two holes the size of half dollars in the bottom of the trunk. Rust had eaten through, so that when he lifted the carpet, the light reflecting from the concrete driveway startled him.

He remembered driving down a street on his way out of town where a water main had broken and flooded the street, forming deep puddles at intersections. The water had splashed the bottom of the car and wicked its way through the carpet onto the cardboard boxes full of recruitment materials, rendering useless a layer of flyers advertising the university.

After he discovered the trunk leak, he put his hand on the mats in the rest of the car. The back seat was fine, but the driver's side and especially the passenger side carpets were wet. He dried them in the sun and resolved to take it slow over puddles.

His office mate, George, had other thoughts, though. Jim was driving the two of them to lunch soon after he had dismissed the holes in the bottom of the car from his mind. He forgot to take it slow over a puddle, and when he hit one at a reasonable speed, George happened to be looking at his feet and saw the carpet bubble up as the water pushed from below. George bent over and lifted the carpet to see the street rushing by, inches below the bottom of the car.

"My God!" he yelled. "You could be driving along and drop into the street!"

"Oh, come on," Jim said. "Don't be a wimp. Those are just little rust holes."

"Rust?" George shouted. "The whole bottom's about to go! This car is a death trap."

Jim was surprised at George's caution. This was a guy who regularly went on whitewater rafting journeys in places like the Grand Canyon for weeks at a time. And now he was afraid of a little rust.

A white-faced George made it to lunch and back to the office, where he began a campaign to tease Jim into getting a new car.

Jim would not let anyone, under any circumstances, manipulate him into buying something. So he began to think of a way to repair the leaky spots at the lowest cost.

He visited the auto parts store, where the store clerks were familiar with him. He always fixed or maintained anything he could on the Toyota.

"How can I seal up some holes in the bottom of my car?" he asked Eddy, his favorite auto parts guy.

"You could take it to a body shop and get a seal coat, but it'll cost at least a hundred bucks."

Jim cringed. "I was thinking of just patching the holes myself. There's maybe a total of five holes."

Eddy thought a moment. "You need to get some sheet metal. You might find some pieces at the home improvement store, maybe go to the junk yard and see if there's an old vent-a-hood from someone's stove."

That sounded like too much expense on the one hand and too much research on the other. He let that issue slide for the moment.

"Okay. What do you recommend to adhere the metal?"

"Spray it with this liquid insulator. It's for sound deadening." Eddy shook the spray can so Jim could hear the marble rattling around inside. He walked on down the aisle and picked up a big tube. "But first, you put on some rows of this epoxy and push the metal over the hole. Brace it up and let it dry."

Jim left the store with the two items Eddy recommended.

The metal would be a problem.

Then that evening, taking out the trash, he found the solution. Cat food cans. The sixteen-ounce size.

Since we had five cats at the time, there was no shortage of cat food cans. Back then, they were still made of heavy tin and not the easily crushed aluminum of the small cans sold now.

That Saturday, Jim scooted under the Toyota and examined its underside. He wiped and sanded around the corroded areas. He washed his collection of cat food cans and took out the bottoms. Then he used tin snips to cut down the sides. He mashed them flat and set his toolbox on them to flatten them. Now he called them "patches." No longer cat food cans, they had been elevated to industrial strength auto body repair patches. While he glued them over the holes under his car, traffic slowed down to creep by and stare at his long body in overalls, sticking out from under the car at odd angles, twitching with the effort to position and secure the patches. Then he sprayed the sound deadener in an even layer for each repair.

It took all day, but he finished. George could no longer heckle him about the holes in his car, but he still got plenty of mileage from the cat food cans Jim confessed to using. That car might spring a new leak, but those patches were secure until the Second Coming.

A few months after he traded in the old Toyota, we saw it driving down one of the busier streets in town. The name "Dawn" was stenciled on the back fender.

"That's great," Jim said. "That car makes a great ride for a teenage girl."

I couldn't resist. "I wonder what she would think of the cat food cans."

"Who cares? It's never gonna leak."

IN THE BOWELS OF THE BEASTLY BEHEMOTH BENEATH THE BOTTOM OF THE SINK

Tony Stafford

I turned to scrape the scraps off my plate into the sink when I realized there was no hole to scrape them into. The sink was full of water and—stuff, awful looking stuff, I know not what—and thought, I have never eaten anything that looks like this in my life. "Where did this come from," an obviously futile, rhetorical question, spoken to the sludge which had formed itself into the image of a face, obviously some demonic spirit.

Well, I thought, a flip of the switch and the growling beast beneath the sink will devour it all before I'll even have time to retch into the sink to add to the post-modernistic looking mess therein. So, I flip the switch and get a response not unlike my fifth wife's response to my foreplay. Nada. Ummm. What to do. Flipping the switch two hundred more times accomplished nothing. Nada. The beast beneath the sink had either fallen asleep or died, in either case of which action was called for. Is there such a thing as a "Beast Beneath the Sink Fixer" in the Yellow Pages? Nada.

∗ ∗ ∗ ∗ ∗ ∗ ∗

"Grrrrrrr! Grrrrrr! and everything vibrates when it's on." I was trying to explain to the clerk in the home repair store what I needed but couldn't think of the word.

"The dishwasher?" he lamely asked.

"No, not the dishwasher. Grrrrrrrrrrr. Rattle, rattle, rattle. Shake, shake shake."

"The trash compacter?"

"No, not the trash compacter. I don't own one of those. Grrrrrrrrrrrrrrrrrrrrrr." I dramatically imitated the damn thing.

"A vibrator?" he whispered.

"No, that's in the bedroom. It's underneath the sink and you feed it food and it eats it up. What's that called?"

"A garbage disposal?" suggested the clerk as he brightened up.

"That's it. That's the beast beneath the sink. Do you carry those?"

"Try aisle eight—kitchen appliances." I did not appreciate the smirk on his face. "Don't you think you ought to call a plumber?" he lamely suggested. How does this guy keep his job, insulting customers like that, I thought.

"Do you have any idea what plumbers cost these days?" giving him my parting shot as I went in search of aisle eight.

"So that's what they look like," I mumbled to myself

as I sauntered around aisle eight and finally found a sign that said "Garbage Disposal" underneath this object that looked like a very large thermos bottle.

"Can I help you with something?" the Earl of Aisle Eight approached me.

"Yeah. I need one of these," I answered, pointing to the thermos bottle.

"Right there in those boxes," he said, pointing to the boxes that had "garbage disposal" written on them.

"Great," I said, as I tried to lift one into my cart and almost dropped it, startled by it heaviness. "Are they all this heavy?"

"You have one of the lighter ones. Are you going to try to install this yourself?"

"Try? Pooh. I've installed hundreds of them. What's the big deal?" I tried to sound like I knew what I was doing as I straightened my body to its full height and lifted my chest cockily higher.

"I think you better call a plumber," the Earl of Aisle Eight offered.

"Another wise ass," I said to myself as I pushed my cart forward. "How does this store stay in business insulting its customers all day long?"

* * * * * * *

CARRASSHH!!!! The old, nonworking beast beneath the sink, a.k.a, the large thermos bottle, came loose and fell to the cabinet floor as I loosened the last screw, already having disconnected it from electricity and plumbing, which was really quite simple. It was a matter of unplugging the electric cord and unscrewing the rubber hose. The old behemoth stood momentarily and then turned over on its side. Gurgle, gurgle, gurgle, it said as it began to unload its contents, odoriferous, greasy, hideous-looking liquid all over the kitchen floor.

✷ ✷ ✷ ✷ ✷ ✷ ✷

"Maybe I should call a plumber," I sighed after two hours of sopping, scraping, and mopping. "Nah, the worst is behind me now," I concluded as I tried to lift the new monster out of the box. "Holy cow, this thing is heeeeaaavvvvy," as I finally turned the box over on its side to slide "The Thing" out of its carton.

I looked at the empty space beneath the sink and then back at the monster and then back at the empty space and then back at the monster and then back at the space and then—several hundred more times. "How in the hell am I going to lift this thing into that space, hold it there while I attach the screws, get the screwdriver, then—I'll need at least eight arms to do all that simultaneously."

I sat on the kitchen floor while I contemplated my dilemma. "I could start by going to the gym and lifting weights until I can—nah, that would take at least a year before I'd be strong enough to hold it in place with one hand while attaching the screws with the other."

"Let me think. I could screw in some hooks to the bottom of the kitchen cabinet just above the sink, add some pulleys, get a strong rope, put the rope through the sink, tie it to the monster, and—what if the cabinet falls, or the rope breaks, or—not feasible."

I thought some more. "Humm. One of the great

inventions of human civilization is the lever, leverage, the fulcrum, power-lift the damn thing right up there into place."

* * * * * * *

Several hours later and after a hundred futile attempts to balance the damn thing on a long pole, I abandoned the idea of the lever, leverage, the fulcrum, human progress, man the machine maker, civilization, modern science, the existential leap, eternal salvation— the whole works. The only logical conclusion, outcome, destiny, result—the summation of the universe—was despair. Suicide even seemed like—"No, don't even go there. Before I'd do that, I'd call a plumber."

The male ego is a strange creature. I mean, how much would a plumber really cost? But it's not the money. It's a point of pride. "So, ok, pride, go to work. But first go to bed." It was the middle of the night by this point in time.

It was not an easy night, full of grotesque dreams and horrid nightmares in a clammy bed. But out of the storm and tempest came a lightning bolt of inspiration. What popped into my head was the image of the inside of the trunk of my car, and in the dark corner of the trunk lay a car jack and the crank that goes with it. "If a car jack can lift a two-ton car. . . " I jumped out of bed, grabbed my car keys from my dresser, and rushed to the garage, clad in pajamas and barefooted. I popped the trunk lid, grabbed the jack and the attendant crank (I'm not referring to myself), and returned to the kitchen, my sacred instruments of salvation in my hands like a knight of old facing a dragon—or, better yet, like a pilgrim reaching the Holy Land.

I placed the jack on the floor of the lower cabinet beneath the drain in the sink. I rolled the new beast to the front of the cabinet, exerted with all my strength to lift the new behemoth onto the little platform on top of the jack, steadied it there, inserted the crank into its proper slot, and began to crank it oh-so-slowly as the beast began to rise oh-so-slowly into the space beneath the drain, like some creature rising into outer space until it reached the lip of bottom of the drain. I connected and tightened the screws, plugged in the electrical cord, attached the rubber hose to its proper place, turned on the faucet to check for leaks, turned on the growling beast and tested its voraciousness with a piece of bread. I lowered the car jack with a counter-clockwise turn of the crank and held my breath. Everything stayed in place.

I laid my male ego to rest, finally. The next day was Saturday, and, in the glow of success, I slept until noon. And gloated.

MAKING ALLOWANCE
Carl "Papa" Palmer

Pleased with my brand new door lock knobs, chrome, smooth, tapered, anti-theft, no ridge to grasp with a coat hanger, I swing shut the door to my truck – with the keys dangling from the ignition. Knowing the doors are locked, I check both sides anyway. Looking through the windows, I pull both handles once more.

Noticing the driver side window slightly down, I snake in a straightened coat hanger. The knob works as advertised.

Tapping the glass with a bumper jack handle, preparing to break the window and file an insurance vandalism claim, my ten-year-old daughter steps into the garage. "Kathy, stand back."

After telling her of my dilemma, I listen as my little girl speaks, "I have an idea, Dad."

I watch her unspool an arm length of nylon fishing line through the opening to touch the knob, squeeze super glue to bubble down the string and form around the knob.

We wait the prescribed one minute, and one to grow on, before she slowly pulls the string to pop the knob and me right out of my predicament.

"Wow! That was terrific! Thanks, Kathy"

"That's all right, Dad, could I please have a dollar advance on my allowance?"

I give her the dollar, and one to grow on.

HOW I CURED MY INSOMNIA WITH DUCT TAPE, A MILK CRATE, A PAIR OF OLD RUNNING SHOES, AND AN EARTH SCIENCE TEXTBOOK

Katie Eber

It's one in the morning and I haven't had a good night's sleep in about a week. For almost a year now, one corner of my bed slowly sunk into the soft membrane of duct tape that held together the shattered plastic of the bed riser adding an extra six inches of lift. Every night as I heaved my drunk, exhausted, or lazy meat sack of a body into my bed, the duct tape stretched and gave a little, like a fine pizza dough.

I can't remember exactly when, but recently, I sat on that weak corner to finish a text to someone I might still be friends with (a lot of my friendships are just holding that title right now) and the whole contraption just gave way. Afterwards, my bed looked like a three-legged pointer insistent that there's a wounded fowl in my bottom dresser drawer.

So after a late dinner, four loads of laundry cleaned and folded, and a batch of rice and beans prepared for the week, I decided to temporarily fix the problem.

See, I can't just buy a new bed riser because then I'd have to buy a set of bed risers, not to mention that the odds of me finding a set of risers that are the exact height of the ones currently under my bed is about the same chance that Elvis is actually still alive and performing in a Dolly Parton Tribute drag show in a suburb of Little Rock.

Getting started, I pulled my milk crate "shoe organizer" that's pretty much filled with a lonely ecosystem of single-shoe organisms and propped up the bed enough to pull the riser (and the wheel of the bed foot) out of the duct tape mess. Failing to extract the wheel from the garbled plastic hunk that was previously a perfectly manufactured modification for where man failed to plan for underbed storage options, I shoved the bit into the hole and slid the plastic underneath.

Without the wheel, that leg was about three inches too short. I needed something pretty thick and pretty sturdy to fix this problem. That's when I saw the textbook on the floor in front of my bookshelf.

Glacial and Quaternary Geology, written by Richard Foster Flint and published in 1971, continues to be the foremost textbook on the subject of glaciers and rocks from about 2.5 million years ago to now.

The text is 906 pages, weighs about 3 pounds and is about 2.5 inches thick. Its hardcover is forest green and sports a gold embossed mastodon. The book has a unanimous 5-star rating from users at Amazon.com and can be purchased for $6.56 + Shipping and Handling. It also makes a great substitute for a wheel missing from a bedframe.

With the height problem solved, I moved onto the issue of the gigantic hole in the center of the bed riser where the wheel punched through. To combat this, I jammed an old running shoe, the mate of which has been missing for a while, onto the foot of the bed and balanced the sole across the lip of the riser. The bed is now leveled almost perfectly.

Hopefully this newfound horizontal stasis will rid me of the incorrigible dreams I've had, the ones that wake me up in the dead of night and take a bit to shake off. They are those dreams – the kind that are fully disconcerting and make you question the true motives of those you love and their earthly souls.

Who is that faceless person chasing you through the international terminal of Dulles?

Who is the one naked in your high school's pool?

What is the meaning of wrestling crocodiles in the desert?

If nothing else, I know I've found an answer, so these questions are just another problem to solve.

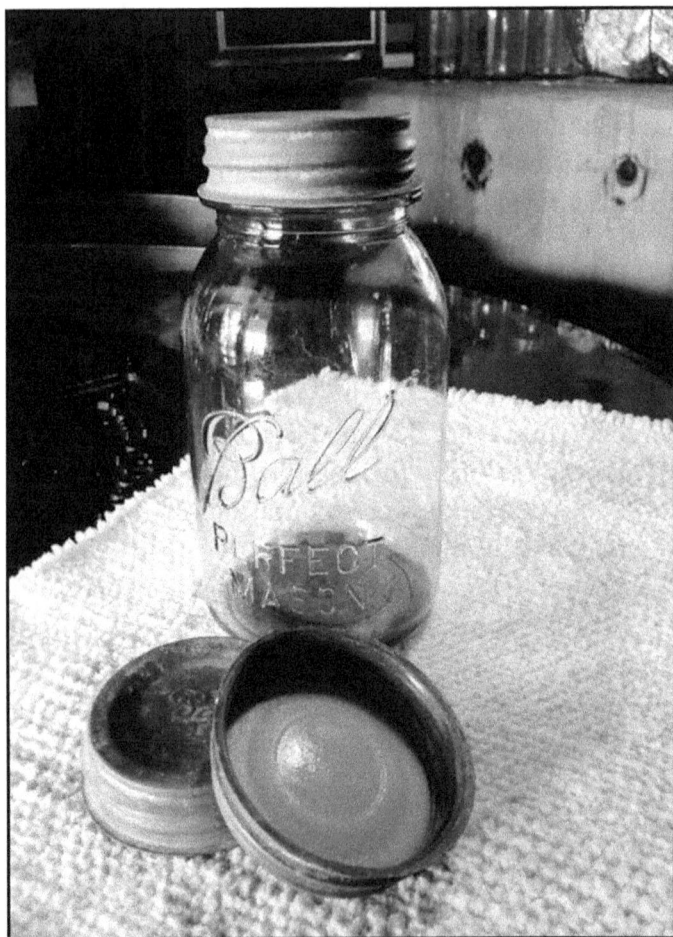

EVERYTHING EXCEPT THE SQUEAL

Margaret and Mitchell Malpass

Americans have lived "high on the hog" since Colonial times.

Hogs were devoured from their heads (scrapple, jowls boiled with vegetables, tongue, and brains with scrambled eggs) to their tails, dunked in stews as a seasoning. Not to mention pigs feet which were baked over hot coals to remove the hooves, then roasted.

Hogs were allowed to range freely in the woods once an owner's brand was cut in their ears, foraging until late November on acorns and chestnuts. They were rounded up and penned for two weeks to fatten on corn before being slaughtered.

Rural Americans butchered and preserved their domestically grown or hunted meat for later use. This laborious task was accomplished by salting, smoking, some winter freezing and/or drying. The Industrial Revolution introduced an additional option – canning in metal cans and glass jars. Glass jars with glass tops soon became standardized, which greatly improved this method.

A further innovation was the development of zinc screw-on lids. These lids were designed with threads and tapered edges, which provided an airtight fit.

Especially in the Midwest and South, pork was a staple meat. As every part of the pig/hog was used "except the squeal," the preparation of the meat was work-intensive. One of the most difficult steps was the removal of the coarse hairs from the pigskin.

A clever person came upon the idea of using the sharp edge of the jar top as a scraper. After the animal was scalded to a precise degree, the worker would grasp the top and use it much like a knife's blade. The "new tool" was probably more comfortable and safer to use than a knife. Another innovation was added: a wooded handle was screwed to the jar top at a perpendicular angle. This provided a firmer grip and added dexterity to the scraper. These ingenious tools are still in use today!

Nowadays when "little piggys" go to the supermarket, it's easy to forget how much effort went into putting meat on the table in times past.

TOOLS
Carl "Papa" Palmer

When I'm unable to get the lid off
a jar of dill pickles, Dad hands me
the same bent butter knife he used
earlier to pry open his key ring.

A toolbox tray in the utility room
has a few rusted nails, some wire,
two hacksaw blades, an ink pen,
several sockets and a toothbrush.

There's a pair of vise grip pliers,
three flat tips and a cross point in
the kitchen drawers I'd seen while
searching for a roll of scotch tape.

Dad had tools in the barn, car trunk
and well house he could never find,
that one of us kids must have used
and didn't back where it belonged.

I arrive to borrow a hammer from my
brother's organized garage filled with
tools for every job, find him scraping
mud from his shoe with a butter knife.

THE DRYER LINT CHRONICLES
Lisa Timpf

As I swung open the dryer door, I was met by a blast of warm, moist air. The dampness of the clothing confirmed what I suspected: the dryer was still not performing its job properly.

We'd asked the seller to include the appliances as part of the "deal" when we purchased our house. In the dryer's case, this wasn't turning out to the best idea ever. The device persisted in returning clothes moist, if not wringing wet, regardless of the setting used or time length applied.

It was time for action.

The first issue we discovered was that the vent pipe hookup within the dryer had become detached. This gave the damp air no place to go, creating a closed-loop recipe for failure. Armed with screwdrivers, we accessed the dryer's inner workings and fixed that little problem using foil tape.

We suspected lint buildup in the dryer vent pipe leading to the outdoors to be a second contributing factor to the appliance's less-than-optimal performance. Fortunately, a section of the dryer vent pipe was accessible in an open-ceiling storage area in the basement.

Once access was gained, we peered down the dark tube with the aid of a flashlight. Just as we suspected, lint had accumulated inside the vent pipe rather like fat deposits on a heart attack candidate's arteries.

Some cursory internet research revealed that there were job-specific dryer-vent-cleaning tools available for purchase, ranging from a power drill attachment to vacuum-type affairs. But what was the fun in that? Besides, buying a kit would mean one more thing to store, and we were trying to downsize. This, by definition, implied restricting the purchase of new tools.

A search of the house turned up a substitute device in the form of a narrow-headed mop left behind by the home's previous owner. The mop head fit snugly into the dryer vent pipe as if designed for that task. A five-foot section of one-by-two wood repurposed from its previous function was strapped to the mop's handle using the handyperson's favorite helper, duct tape, and we were in business.

Okay, that got us about eight feet down the pipe. Now what?

We resorted to attaching successive five-foot lengths of one-by-twos using duct tape, and using them as a handle to push the mop head through the dryer pipe, hoping fervently that the entire contraption wouldn't come apart as snaked its way down the pipe toward the outdoor termination of the vent. It was an inelegant but effective solution. When the yellow mop head finally appeared in the light of day, it was preceded by a satisfyingly large lint mass which we quickly bundled up for disposal.

Section by section, we hauled the remainder of the makeshift "handle" out of the dryer vent, then taped the vent back together in the basement.

When cleanup from the task was complete, it was time to start the dryer. With fingers crossed, we waited until the perfidious machine indicated its cycle was done.

We'd been fooled before by the green light heralding "clothes dry," so I paused to steel myself before opening the door.

No blast of moist air. And – wonder of wonders – the laundry was warm and dry to the touch. Success!

Since then, the dryer has performed impeccably. And if the day comes when it doesn't – well, we know what to do.

A SEWING BOX WITH A BROKEN LATCH

JoAnna Scandiffio

most people would buy a new box
or let the box be unsecured

who would steal a metal thimble odds & ends
a stocking needle

not my mother she can't let brokenness be

she fastens the latch loop with an old silver key
from a house that held a memory long gone to sea

she uses the key as a horizontal rod
to prevent slippage

                    pins and needles

don't ask how she tried to fix me or my siblings

she gave us her glue her stick-to-it-ness
this keeps us from holes in our socks

but not from falling apart when we lose a
button or a husband

Ben Musick's Invention

If you talk to Ben Musick, Kingfisher, Okla., for ten minutes he'll show you this invention. He took an old oil drum, cut out the head, inserted a tub, attached a wringer and—presto!—you have the neatest chamois cleaner you ever saw. Ben is a great Dixie Booster and a fine fellow besides. The Musick Oil Co., justifiably enjoys a splendid business in Kingfisher.

THE NEATEST YOU EVER SAW
Jack L. Musick & Kathleen Musick Gancer

In the early 1930s it was necessary to be resourceful and frugal in every part of your life during the Great Depression. Our father owned and operated a gasoline service station in his small hometown of Kingfisher, Oklahoma, as well as being a farmer. He was skilled at solving problems by piecing together tools from parts of discarded machines.

Among other things, he invented a hydraulic greasing rack, which made all parts of a car easily accessible. However, the tool he created that rated a story and photo in *The Kingfisher Times and Free Press* was for wringing out chamois cloths. He cut off the head of an old oil drum and put a tub in it. Then he attached a wringer to the tub so a chamois could be washed easily after each use. The *Times* called it, "the neatest chamois cleaner you ever saw!"

SCREWDRIVER MATHEMATICS
Carl "Papa" Palmer

Lying up under the car
on the floor of the garage
I see his little feet arrive,
the shadow of his head
bending down to ask,
"Whattaya want, Dad?"

"Hand me that number two Phillips
on the workbench over there, son."

I watch him switch his weight
from one little foot to the other,
step away, start back, stop,
turn around and then
scamper back to the car,
leaning lower to ask,
"Dad, is the Phillips a plus or a minus?"

THE ZIPPER

Patty J. Crocker, M.D.

Mr. Smith* was the sickest patient on the trauma service — and now, on the first day of my last year of medical school, he became my primary responsibility. He had been admitted as a Level One trauma victim three weeks earlier, and he had already had as many surgeries. As I reviewed his chart, I saw he was now spiking another fever, so I knew I would likely be scrubbing in on his 4th operation soon.

When your doctor is a surgeon, your treatment is probably going to be surgical. There were several labs and imaging studies pending to look for the source of his fever, but if nothing was found then he would be scheduled to undergo an exploratory surgery. Mr. Smith was a 60-year-old man in critical condition since his car accident nearly a month prior. On a road trip with several family members, he had just switched from driver to front seat passenger in order to lean back the seat and get some rest. EMS reports stated everyone else in the car was awake and sitting up when the tragic event occurred.

The pictures of the car in Mr. Smith's chart showed a large sedan that had the front end pushed into the passenger compartment, and damage to all 4 sides from rolling over. Saturday night in northwestern New Mexico is not the best time to traverse the Native American reservation on Interstate 40. Emergency medical services are limited as they are provided by local rural volunteer fire departments, not from highly-trained, full-time paramedics like in big cities.

At three am, a drunk driver crossed the median and struck Mr. Smith's car, killing every person involved except him. Sadly, he was the only person wearing a seatbelt when the collision happened — and he was lying on his back with the front passenger seat fully reclined, sound asleep. Unfortunately, the seatbelt that saved his life also pushed his intestines up into his chest, rupturing his diaphragm and breaking ribs which punctured his lungs in the process, due to his recumbent position.

He had several other fractures, lacerations, contusions and abrasions, but the worst injuries involved the internal organs in his chest and abdomen. After a helicopter ride to the University of New Mexico, the only Level One trauma hospital in the state, his first operation was performed immediately upon his arrival.

After having tubes placed in his chest to treat the punctured lungs, his intestines were pulled back into his belly and his ruptured diaphragm repaired. The intestines were too swollen to allow his skin to be closed, so sterile surgical towels were packed into the surgical wound before admitting him to the ICU. A few days later, after most of the swelling subsided, he was taken back to the OR for another look-see. Nothing of note was found, just some small bleeders which were cauterized, and the skin was pulled closed with sturdy wire sutures to allow his abdominal wall to begin healing.

In the week prior to my joining the trauma service, Mr. Smith spiked his first fever, and after other infections were ruled out, he went for his third operation. His wound was reopened not with a scalpel, but by the surgeon sticking a finger into the wound and basically tearing the partially-healed surgical incision open. This is a standard surgery technique, called "blunt dissection" — unlike sharp dissection, which is with a knife or scissors.

The rough ripping and tearing always seemed brutal to me, but using a scalpel would cause more damage by slicing bits of tissue which would then become dead material in the wound, a nice source of food for any bacteria lurking around. After finding a small abscess by a bit of dead gut, last week the surgeons cleaned everything up and once again closed the wound, but left drains to monitor any fluids that might start developing around the surgical site.

Drains can be removed without opening the surgical wound, so once again his abdominal skin was being allowed to grow back together at the site of surgery. Now, as the labs and imaging studies were completed, it appeared he had not a problem with the injury, but an infected gallbladder which was causing the new fever. This is not uncommon with a patient under extreme stress, so trauma surgeons encountered this problem from time to time.

Back then, the only treatment was surgical removal of the gallbladder. Intravenous antibiotics were mainly fighting spread of infection but not expected to cure it. Endoscopy was just beginning to be used in the operating room, and some mature surgeons felt it was a novelty that wouldn't last very long. Of course, those same surgeons also thought cautery was an abomination and continued to spend countless hours in the OR tying off bleeders!

On rounds that morning, it was mentioned that the same incision was to be bluntly reopened as the gallbladder could easily be reached through the existing surgical incision and another wound would just be another opportunity for infection. When this was being discussed, I jokingly suggested sewing a nylon zipper onto the edges of his wound to make easier access for the next likely event.

The patient seemed to be getting every surgical complication in the book, and critical trauma patients sometimes have a dozen or more surgeries in the first few months of recovery. To my surprise, instead of hearing laughter, the two very young attending physicians (teaching doctors) started discussing the idea. A drug rep visiting the ICU had recently handed out cheap plastic fanny packs with nylon zippers, and a few unused ones were still lying on a nearby counter. I was given the go ahead to get the fanny pack down to the sterilization room to be gassed (sterilized without heat) and labeled for our team.

The preparation for Mr. Smith's fourth trip to the OR was uneventful. After his gallbladder was removed, the anesthesiologist and nurses couldn't believe what they were witnessing when the attending surgeon Dr. Jones* cut the zipper from the fanny pack, then with a bit of Gortex to back the plastic, sewed it onto each side of the wound.

The reactions of the ICU nurses were equally amusing. After they recovered from the shock, they found it useful for dressing changes as they didn't have to put tape on his rather hairy skin! The six days he had the zipper resulted in a troop of visitors who had to see this curiosity for themselves.

My attending physicians also received quite a bit of notoriety on campus for their daring surgical feat. Alas, Mr. Smith soon returned emergently to the operating room, again for more dead bowel, so the zipper was removed and sent to the lab for culture to see if it was bacteria-laden. Since it takes twenty-four hours to gas sterilize a heat-sensitive item like plastic, we never were able to try again to place a zipper in Mr. Smith – who, after eight months in the hospital and rehabilitation, survived and never even knew he was my most memorable patient.

*Names changed for privacy

Thinking Outside the Toolbox

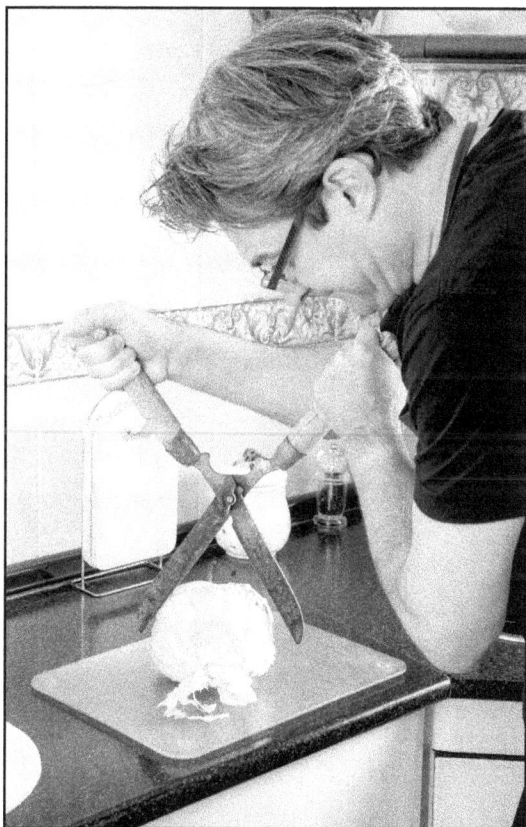

BE MINE

Carole Ann Moleti

A working mother's life runs like a clock. Even a tiny blip can shatter the crystal and send the mechanism into a deadlocked spasm. I'd taken the day off to pitch my novel to a panel of editors and agents in Manhattan—a gut-twisting experience in the best of circumstances. Making the early train and getting the kids off to school wasn't going to make it any less so.

I woke my daughter up to help her get dressed before I left, and was horrified to note a single chickenpox. No fever, but she was wiggling her chin like a hag. Even though it had to be the reaction I was warned about when Maya got her vaccination two weeks prior, I knew she'd never be allowed to stay in school.

My husband took one look at it, then at me in my suit. "Just go. I'll stay home. The boys have their concert tonight, and it would be next to impossible to get them there on time anyway."

"Are you sure you can do that?" Guilt stabbed my gut, and this delay was going to mean I wouldn't have time to grab a coffee and muffin before getting on the train.

"I'll work remotely. Let me drive you to the station or you won't make it." He screamed upstairs, warning the boys they'd better be up and dressed when he got back.

I bundled my daughter into her jacket, grabbed my briefcase and coat, and got into the car for the three-minute drive. When I jumped out one leg seemed shorter than the other.

"Good luck." My husband drove off.

I took one step and almost fell. The heel on my right boot was gone. Nowhere to be found. For one split second I imagined I could just walk on the ball of the foot, then remembered the ten-block sprint I had to make from Penn Station to Ripley-Greer Studios.

"Wait!" I was able to get my husband's very divided attention and jump back in. "I need to change shoes and get back here in five minutes to make the train."

Tense silence filled the car. The gears were about to blow. "Keep the car running." The boys had the front door open, and I blasted past them.

"Get in the car and wait for me." I raced upstairs, tunneled in my closet for an older pair of scuffed but serviceable boots, and was back in two minutes. Still one to spare.

I try and stay on the good side of karma, thinking very carefully about sarcastic comments and selfish actions, such as dumping a sick child on an unwitting father, then making him drive circles around the neighborhood to help a crazed woman make a train while the kids sat in stunned silence in the back seat. The caffeine withdrawal headache punched me behind the eyes while I worried that Maya would be feverish and fussy.

But the karmic glitch in the gears resolved itself. Though the tote board said "on time" the train was three minutes late, and I even got a seat. My heartbeat slowed down to normal on the twenty-minute ride. After a ten minute walk, I got to Ripley-Greer, got a coffee and muffin, and found my seat in the conference room where me and about fifteen other aspiring novelists would be coached and briefed before facing down the jaws of the literary sharks.

* * * * * * *

No sales, but I'd gotten helpful feedback. I closed the door on that compartment and opened the next. The clock kept ticking along, but the boys would be at the concert even if I was late. Sure I'd be hungry, but life is full of hardships.

The train was on time, I had two heels on my nice comfy boots, and the porch lights twinkled a welcome. As the door creaked open, anguished cries met my ears.

"I can't find my red bow tie!"

"Where did you put it?" My husband can't find milk in the refrigerator so I headed upstairs, sure it was under the bed or stuffed in a drawer.

"Where I always put it!"

"Then where did it go?" The sound of my husband moving furniture jammed a screwdriver into the karmic gears.

My daughter and middle son Adam stood staring at Nicholas and their father tearing the room apart.

"Nicky can't find his bow tie, Mommy." The pustule on Maya's chin was covered with a band-aid, and she looked just fine.

"Mommy's here." I bypassed my husband pawing through the closet, tossing shoes, socks and Legos over his shoulder.

"Get me the dust mop!" It appeared, and I swiped under the beds and furniture.

Nick had dumped every drawer into the middle of the room and there was no red flash in the pan.

The gears were jammed, and I was out of ideas.

"I can't show up without a bow tie. Doc will kill me."

My middle son has impeccable comic timing and good sense. "You're making me late and then Doc will kill us both. Let's go. Hide your neck until we sit down and then just keep your trombone up high."

"Doc sees everything." Nick was still jamming the gears.

I ran into my bedroom to see if my husband had any misplaced red amongst his ties, and my eyes went immediately to the teddy bear he'd given me one Valentine's Day perched atop my alarm clock. His bright red bow was covered up by a large, white patch begging to "Be Mine" but if the tie fits...

"Nick, come here." I grabbed my sewing kit, cut the ribbon off Teddy's neck, and snipped the patch off the tie.

"I'm not wearing that." He gave me that "I'd rather Doc kill me" look.

"It's red, and you're in the back of the stage playing a trombone. No one will notice it's fake. Now get over here." I put the last stich in place and safety-pinned Teddy's naked tie to either side of Nick's shirt.

"This looks ridiculous," he protested.

"It looks fine. Let's go," Adam insisted.

"Mommy, Teddy misses his bow." My daughter cradled the bear.

"I'll put it back on him tonight. Bring him along so he can see his tie. Let's go."

"I can't believe this," my husband said.

I couldn't either.

Nick was the last to slip into his chair next to the other trombones, chin tucked into his chest until he raised the instrument to his lips. Doc, acting as conductor, tapped his wand, scanned the orchestra and found everyone ready.

I must have been a very good girl.

CUSTODIENNE

Barbara E. Kirchner

With reference to lamps and doors,
And faucets, irons, or squeaking floors,
I used to wait upon my spouse
To fix these things around the house.
But, soon it fell to me, alone,
To call up on the telephone
Plumbers, glaziers, electricians
To perform these urgent missions.

To my chagrin and shrinking purse,
What should have worked kept getting worse!
But, lo! I found a priceless tome
On how to fix things in the home.
I now rewire, repair, rebuild
With all the wisdom of the skilled.

For benefit of men who think
That ladies cannot fix a sink;
Beware a cunning, cheerful wench

Who's learned to utilize a wrench.
It's easy to replace a fuse
Or hammer nails, or screw the screws;
Apply the pliers, or tighten nuts,
While loathing all repairmen's guts —
Fantasizing, I pretend
That they are on the other end.

ROUGH NIGHT AT SEA
Richard Ford

Well, not at sea, really. Not the real sea. It was Lake Michigan.

But for me it was the perilous North Atlantic and our modest yacht, on a dark and stormy night, was tempest tossed in the grandest tradition of a Johnson Oatman hymn ("When upon life's billows you are tempest tossed, When you are discouraged, thinking all is lost, Count your many blessings...") or an Emma Lazarus sonnet ("Give me your tired, your poor, Your huddled masses yearning to breathe free, The wretched refuse of your teeming shore. Send these, the homeless, tempest-tost to me..."). But forgive my rambling; I had "harbored" delusions of literary grandeur from an early age.

The yacht "slept eight but laid sixteen," my dad confided to me when mom was not around, with a curl of his eyebrows and a wink I thought I understood. Should I wink back? Probably. I was fourteen.

My dad was a furniture buyer for Sears. His friend, a manufacturer of bedding and owner of the yacht, was courting my dad that summer. My dad's business, you understand, along with that of one of my dad's associates, Max, the mattress tycoon, and his wife, Elaine, had promised us — my folks and me, along with Dad's colleague and his wife and son Wayne — a trip around the lake: up the western shore northward from Chicago, two nights in Mackinaw, with stops at Charlevoix and other places I don't even remember. Almost a week in all, and it was all a revelation to me – I had never been boating nor eaten so much seafood in such a short time.

What I do remember, and will never forget, is the dark and stormy night.

Red-haired, self-possessed Elaine was kind and wise, a doting Jewish mother whose own son happened not to be on board with us, alas. Wayne or I would have to suffice.

The night of the gale, the rain was suddenly torrential. The yacht leapt and lurched. Just moments earlier, I had donned my pajamas, but staying in bed was going to be a tricky proposition, what with the vessel being buffeted about like a matchstick. My lunch was safe, but my dinner clearly was not. I grabbed my tummy and groaned a grievous groan. My eyes struggled not to swim.

Wayne's only emotion was excitement, damn him. For him it was an adventure.

Elaine perceived the true extent of my distress and, holding tight with one hand to a fixture on the wall, made me a tempting offer.

"Dick, wait a minute! I've got some Dramamine in my purse. Motion sickness pills. I always bring them along."

She rummaged through her bag for at least a minute and finally produced a pill, which she clasped in my hand.

"Here. Now take this right away. And don't swallow it. Just suck on it. Suck on it hard till it's all gone. Let it dissolve slowly, so the medicine will take full effect. All right? It doesn't taste good, but that's how you know it's working!"

Right. I sucked and sucked, and it did taste pretty awful, but for me it was a soothing lozenge, a chalky LifeSaver without a hole. The awfuler it tasted, the better I felt. Pretty soon my head hit the pillow and I was falling asleep.

The next morning was calm and sunny. I awoke to my mom and Elaine's concerned questions. I was fine.

"Elaine, thank you so much," I gushed. "I thought I would be really sick."

Wayne said I still looked a little green.

"You're welcome, boy. Glad you're feeling better. But you know? This must be the only time I've ever forgotten to bring along my Dramamine! All I had in my purse was some breath mints and a little bottle of decongestant cold tablets, so I just handed you a Dristan. I thought if I told you to concentrate on sucking it and how bad it tasted you might forget about the rest."

My mom laughed and said, "Mind over matter, eh?"

Feeling both embarrassed and delighted to have been deceived, I laughed, too.

A MOVING POEM

Jen Wynkoop

Yesterday was move-in day
over on Eighteenth Street.
Into a five-floor walk-up from a three-floor walk-
down
in New York's July heat.
The couch came down in pieces—
all arms and cushions and pallets.
The box spring was another story:
shouts of "Pivot!" and "Do you have it?"
Things were OK for a while,
until it came time to move
that damn old tube TV set
State of the art!…in '92.
Too wide to wrap your arms around.
Too heavy for less than three.
Much too old for HDMI,
but hand-me-downs are free!
For a while we puzzled over
the monster in my room

and the pre-war spiral staircase
we feared would be our doom.
"Well, why don't we just roll it?
As in, end over end?
Slowly down we'll go
and pause at every bend."
So we put our plan to action
and slowly down we went
heaving the 200-pound relic, and
producing many new dents.
The rest of the move moved smoothly.
Doubtless, the others agree:
Bryan's fingers slammed in the door jam,
and a bookcase sliced Kel's knee.
The mattress on top of the Jeep
was "secured" with old jump ropes.
Tack holes in the bedroom wall were filled with
white toothpaste (and bygone deposit hopes).
Into the new building we go!
Moving up through the front doors
—up and up and up and up—
"Why are there so many floors?!"
Dee gave up on the dresser
between the fourth and fifth floor gap.
Panting, cross-legged on the stairs,
she cried, "I need a freaking nap!"
Once again, this tube TV
presented a difficult matter.
Sure, rolling down was simple enough,
but, up? Gravity factors.
So I called my big, big brother
(six-feet-four and a good weight-lifter)

what else could he really say?
Of course, he'd help his sister!
When Matt arrived I gestured with pride
toward the obstacle that remained.
He frowned and sighed and simply replied,
"This is going to be a pain."
Without a real plan to speak of
he hefted it up a few inches.
I sat down by the bannister;
"Watch out for finger pinches!"
That little, vertical lift
proved well enough indeed.
With Bryan, he slid it, bumping up,
at a snail's breakneck speed.
When they finally reached my door
(what felt like hours later)
I ordered the pizza and opened the beer—
how else to return the favor?
Sweating through my tank, I smiled.
"That wasn't so bad," I said.
The grim faces of my friends replied,
"We wish that you were dead."

SO MUCH HAS HAPPENED
Ibeji Grace

I heard my father's voice calling me when I came. He said he's got something he wanted to tell me. I told him I was all ears. Then he said he's not my biological father. I was shocked. Then I asked him whom my biological father was. He mentioned the shoemender next door.

"What? The shoemender next door? Not even someone who's financially stable?" I asked in my mind. Then I cried. I cried not only because I loved my father, but also that my real father was a poor man. Haba! Is this not entering from frying pan to fire?

Just then I heard a faint voice calling my name from far away. It was my mother. She woke me up. Then I realized it was a dream, but I didn't tell anyone about it. They'd say it was a malaria dream. I quickly prepared for the journey my elder brother and I were going to embark on. We were going back to Abia, our state of origin.

When all the necessary arrangements had been made, we boarded a vehicle and started our trip. Before then my brother had bought a lot of things ranging from mangoes, banana, meat pies, oranges, coke and many other eatables. I plugged in my earphones and started listening to some songs I had termed "travel songs." Unknown to me, my brother was downloading the things he bought — one after the other. After some time, he tapped me and said he needed to use a restroom urgently.

Without warning I heard a familiar sound. He had released the waste products on himself! My mouth was agape. We stared at each other.

"What are we going to do?" I asked.

I thought very hard and came up with an option. He was wearing trousers, which means if he stood up it was going to rush all the way to his shoes and people will see it.

So we used our earphones to tie his legs separately to prevent it from running out.

"If anybody asks you what this means, tell him it's a swag," I said with a smile.

The rest of the trip was like a dream. Every other thing that happened was not noticed by us. Our minds were centered on reaching home. When at last we arrived, he avoided the little children that came to welcome us and rushed to the bathroom to get cleaned!

Later he came out with a towel wrapped around his waist as Grandma looked on in surprise.

She said, "It seems so much has happened." We couldn't help laughing.

Then I answered, "Yes, Grandma, so much has happened."

Then I looked at my brother with something in my eyes that said, "You'll owe me a lot if I am going to keep your little secret."

Then he nodded.

TORCH

mariana mcdonald

I never had to deal with battery acid,
though flashlights are a staple in my life:
at home stuck to the grumbling icebox,
on the bed nightstand, in the hall.
The chunky ones—a fistful of lighthouse,
round ones twirling like a baton.
Small ones hiding in the glove box,
junk box, toolbox in the car.

A dripping ceiling prompted night
adventure in the attic, kitchen torch
in hand. I didn't notice it was sticky,
viscous. I was focused on the water
making mad Monets along the ceiling.
I finally found the culprit in the bathroom:
a leaky toilet for a plumber to fix.
Set the flashlight on my writing desk

and made the call for help. Next day
I went to pay some bills piled on the table
and saw a trail of white spots near
a circle. Dang. The flashlight. I'd been
clueless of its whereabouts with all
the wet distress. I guess it didn't matter,
the sticky splatter now a dappled mess
I try to hide with marker pen—mahogany.

It had to be the acid in the batteries
that turned the chesnut desk to chalky white,
leaving shallow craters in the wood
like planets pocked from stars' debris,
meteors left by that old torch. It looks
like hell. Oh well. When I write there
I can think of galaxies. The lesson learned:
that when it rains, it can also scorch.

A WOMAN'S SECRET TOOL

Carol Graham

"Mom, I sold the engine mount for my motorbike on eBay. Can you mail it for me?" No problem. Piece of proverbial cake.

I knew the UPS store would package it for me. Purchasing the necessary packing supplies for this irregular parcel, I assumed they would help me do this without incident. I had collected $35 from the eBay customer which, again assuming, would be more than adequate funds. Three wrongs do not make one right!

They told me the parcel would be ready in about half an hour. I went to the post office to mail other items and there was a thirty-minute line up. The post office is a great place to watch people deal with stress. For some reason, apparently the person standing behind the counter is at TOTAL FAULT for a parcel being lost in transit. It is also that employee's fault that the cost of postage is so high!

Realizing how stressful their job can be, I usually get the employees laughing. Wicket number one is Joe. He is bald, retiring soon and has a handlebar mustache that he plays with consistently — probably a stress reliever. Ken, in wicket number two, is a very short man who thinks he is an Elvis impersonator and usually starts serenading me when he sees me come through the door. I try to ignore him, and he just sings louder until I acknowledge him, with at least a nod. Is this a way for him to deal with his stressful day? Then there is Jim. He is a very good looking man with long curly gray hair. He is the most serious of the group.

My lucky day — I get Jim. We chat for a minute, and one of the workers in the back recognizes my voice and comes out to say hello. This certainly makes up for all the time spent waiting in line, and I joke with them both for a minute and get them laughing.

Now, back to the UPS store to mail the parcel. The girl who waited on me sighs a big sigh and says, "Sorry, but I had to put three boxes together to accommodate the crank sticking out on the side and the cost is $20 to prepare it for shipping."

"No problem." I knew that I had collected $35 for shipping and figured I had plenty for postage. I asked for the cheapest rate, and after checking them all, she said, "$120 is the cheapest."

"Excuse me?" I assumed I did not hear her correctly and asked her to repeat it. Nope, heard her right. At this point, I decided to try the post office as I "hoped" she would be wrong.

Now that the engine mount was in a box, it would not fit into the back of my Jeep. The thermometer outside was rapidly rising. I was trying to manipulate this monstrosity into my SUV and finally managed, but with a third of it sticking out the back window. It was over eight feet long.

Back to the post office. After waiting in line FORTY minutes, with a box that is taller than me, Ken waits on me. He starts to sing about how long it has been since he last saw me, laughing because it was just earlier that day! I'm tired and hot and want to get this done!

He points out that a metal part has punctured the box and is sticking out the side. "Sorry, but you can't mail it in this condition. You will have to fix it and bring it back."

Thanking him I said, "OK, but can you tell me how much it will cost to mail it?"

He measures it and says, "$120." I felt like asking him is he was on glue, but I held my composure. "If you are able to scrape two inches off the package, it will only cost $35."

A kind gentleman helped me get the box into my vehicle and I headed back to the UPS store. Explaining the situation to the gal, we decided we would make this work.

The first problem was to unbolt the crank that was sticking out the side of the box. We both tried to loosen it without any luck. There were no pliers in the store and we had no way to unscrew the rusty crank. An idea hit me. We made a little cardboard "box" to fit around it to cover it completely. Then I explained the problem with the length. We tried to "squish" it shorter. I sat on the box while she strapped it with heavy duty tape. "There, that should do it!" She measured it and it had now grown five inches.

At this point, tears might have come easily but logic had to take over. I could do this. Once again, I didn't believe her and measured it myself. It was only one inch over the limit. She suggested I go back to the post office and cry — maybe the sympathy card would work in my favor.

Load it back into the Jeep. Get in line. THIRTY minutes this time. When the guys saw me in line, there was loud laughter. I was thrilled to have made their day. SURE, it really was funny, but I was not having any fun.

Ken waits on me again. He measures it and I tell him, "I have to mail it for $35." He measures it and says, "Sorry, that will be $200." I must have looked like I was going to burst into tears and he started to laugh loudly. "Actually, you did a great job and it will cost you $29. The part that was sticking out before looked pretty rusty; I was wondering how you were going to unscrew it. Only a woman would think of covering it with cardboard and duct tape."

I smiled. A woman's tenacity was the only tool that was needed.

MONHEGAN
Mark Knobloch

"If we leave now, we should be back at Harborfields around 8:00 tonight," Rick said. "I know you and Mimi have to get up by 5:00 tomorrow morning to go fishing."

The six of us had spent the day visiting friends on Monhegan. The crew included me, my wife Denise, our two daughters and Denise's mother Mimi, who is Rick's wife. Rick was the captain. We had sailed from Harborfields, Rick's family property outside of Boothbay Harbor, Maine, over to Monhegan. The sailboat, Patrician2, was a 44-foot Catalina Morgan, a modern and comfortable cruising sailboat equipped with all of the latest in nautical technology.

Monhegan is a small, rocky island located in the Gulf of Maine, about ten miles from the nearest mainland. The island is scarcely a square mile in area. It is accessible only by boat and there are no cars or paved roads. Since before the explorer John Smith visited it in 1614, it was known to Native Americans as a prime fishing area. Today, its economy is still ruled by fishing and lobstering. The year-round population has seldom exceeded 65 in recent times.

For more than 100 years, Monhegan has been a summer haven for artists and other visitors who appreciate its isolation, the beauty of its wilderness, and its quiet relaxed atmosphere.

The sail over had taken about three hours. There are several ferries that go between Boothbay Harbor and Monhegan, but we thought it would be fun to sail across. Rick had made arrangements to use one of the guest boat moorings in Monhegan Harbor for the day. We spent the day hiking some of Monhegan's trails, often steep and strenuous, that led through wooded areas and over rocky ledges up to the highest ocean cliffs on the Maine coastline. Eventually, we worked our way across the island to Squeaker Cove, on the eastern edge of Monhegan, before returning back to the harbor.

After getting back to the dock, it took several trips rowing our inflatable dinghy between the dock and Patrician2 to get our crew and supplies ready for the return trip to Harborfields. After getting everything situated, Rick said he was ready to start the engine so we could motor out of Monhegan Harbor. Once we had cleared the southern tip of nearby Manana Island, we would then raise the sails. Despite numerous attempts at starting the diesel engine, nothing happened. Rick made several trips between the deck and the engine down below, trying to figure out what was causing the problem. Finally, Rick said he would row back over to the Monhegan dock to see if the harbor master could send a mechanic over to Patrician2. After a while, we saw Rick rowing back towards the boat by himself, with no mechanic in sight. He had reached the harbor master five minutes after they had closed for the day.

Although he was annoyed by the circumstances (especially since he had recently had Patrician2 serviced at the boat yard in Boothbay Harbor) Rick was not concerned at all. He said we could sail out of Monhegan Harbor. It would just take more time, and require a lot of tacking back and forth, before reaching the Gulf of Maine's open water. It would also be challenging because of the light and variable winds in the protected harbor area, not to mention the other boats moored around us.

We all agreed with Rick's plan. When it comes to anything nautical, Rick was considered a master. He grew up sailing the coast of Maine, attended the Webb Institute of Naval Architecture, and spent his entire career in boat design and manufacturing. He was an expert sailor with an uncanny ability to predict wind and weather conditions. On the occasions when things did go wrong, he always had the ability to solve the problems. The rest of us served as Rick's crew when needed, but mostly we relaxed on these trips and enjoyed the benefits of his sailing expertise.

We worked our way through Monhegan Harbor and eventually cleared Manana Island. Now it was just a matter of sailing west towards Boothbay Harbor. At this point, the winds picked up and we were making good progress. It was a clear evening as we began our leisurely sail home.

After a while, Denise, Mimi and the girls went below deck to prepare dinner for everyone. With Rick at the helm, we finished our meal just as the sun was setting beyond the point of Patrician2's bow.

It wasn't long thereafter when we noticed that the wind had diminished significantly. The boat speed reduced by several knots and the water became very calm. Rick didn't seem concerned, saying that it was just a pocket of quiet air that would probably be temporary. So we continued to trudge along under full sail, both the main and the jib.

After a few hours, it was just me and Rick on deck. The rest had gone below to relax in the cabin area. By this point, it was approaching 10:00 at night. It wasn't long before those down below had all fallen asleep. Our expected 8:00 arrival back at Harborfields was well behind us.

Time continued to move forward, seemingly faster than Patrician2. Conditions in the Gulf of Maine were now basically "dead calm." There were no clouds, no wind, no disturbances on the water's surface. And no other boats or coastline within sight. Although Rick was frustrated, he wasn't concerned.

By now it was past midnight. Both Rick and I were getting tired. He suggested that I go below and get some sleep. But I decided to keep him company on deck. There wasn't much to do, just watch the sails lightly flap lazily in the dark and study the stars above.

After a while longer, out of curiosity, I asked Rick what he would do if there was a true emergency and he had to abandon Patrician2. He said he would prepare to leave the boat and then take the dinghy to safety. But that wasn't a possibility now, with six of us on board.

"But," I asked, "how would you get to land in the dinghy if you were stranded out here. That would take a hell of a lot of rowing."

Rick said, "I would use the small outboard motor."

"Motor? What motor?" I asked. Rick told me that he had a 25 horsepower motor down below that could be used with the dinghy.

"So, can we attach the motor to Patrician2 and power the sailboat that way?" I asked.

"No, there isn't a way to secure the motor to the sailboat," Rick replied. The thought of one of us taking the dinghy and motoring ahead to Boothbay Harbor didn't make sense. I wouldn't know where I was going, and Rick needed to stay with Patrician2 as he was the only qualified captain.

"What if we put the motor on the dinghy and used it to push the sailboat?" I asked.

"Wow. That's an interesting idea," Rick replied. "Not sure pushing the boat will work, but we might be able to tow it."

So I took the helm while Rick went down below to get the motor. We agreed that I would climb down into the dinghy, he would pass me the motor, and I would then attach it. The inflatable dinghy was not very large or steady. The riskiest part of the plan would be having me attach the motor while sitting in the dinghy in complete darkness. The thought of making a mistake and realizing that Rick's motor could sink to the bottom of the Gulf of Maine crossed my mind a few times.

Eventually, I was able to secure the motor. Now the question was would it even start. After a few pulls on the starting rope it fired up. Before dropping the propeller in the water and turning the throttle handle, we had to lash the dinghy to the starboard side of Patrician2. Rick decided that this would be the best position for me to sit in the dinghy and power it forward, while he guided the sailboat.

The plan worked. I had to keep the outboard running and the dinghy going straight. Rick was responsible for the real navigation. About every 10 minutes or so, Rick would call out asking if I was okay.

"Fine here. How are you doing?" I would reply.

"Everything is good up here," he would say.

We "dinghy motored" Patrician2 for a few hours, past Pemaquid Point, between Squirrel Island and Linekin Bay, before finally approaching Boothbay Harbor and eventually Harborfields. Docking the boat with our set up would be difficult. The main dock at Harborfields was in a small protected area, around an outcropping of land that is completely submerged when the tide is high. But Rick knew the exact location of all obstacles, having sailed in and out of this area hundreds of times. As we cleared the rocks, Rick told me to cut the engine, untie the dinghy from the side of the boat so that it floated to its position behind Patrician2, and climb back into the sailboat. He felt that he had enough momentum to glide Patrician2 up to the dock and have enough control so that I could then jump from the sailboat to the dock with a line in hand. Sounded simple, right?

Well, Rick pulled it off perfectly. We docked Patrician2, woke up the rest of the crew, and offloaded all of our gear. There wasn't much celebration or story telling, as we were all tired. By the time I climbed into bed, it was around 3:00 in the morning. So much for the 8:00 p.m. estimated arrival. But we had returned safely, with an adventure to remember. The alarm for fishing at 5:00 that morning came quickly, but I made the wake-up call, as did Mimi, and we were back out on the water almost as soon as we had left it.

KEEP YOUR MITTS OFF
Madeleine McDonald

Like my Mum, I have a secret stash of screwdrivers. Mum kept hers in her underwear drawer, along with a meager emergency fund of money saved from her housekeeping allowance. She made regular use of both.

Forty years on and my screwdrivers, along with a few other essential tools, are secreted in a drawer of my filing cabinet. A lifetime of living with a non-handyman has taught me the value of putting tools out of his reach if I want to find them in working order.

My non-handyman is however a gardener, alive to the wonders of nature. The first snowdrops of the year, the tender green of new leaves unfurling on an established houseplant, and the plumpness of ripening vegetables, all fill him with respect and awe. Nothing is too much trouble for the plants he pampers. This is the man who road-tested our new electric lawnmower on an indoor rug. Perish the thought that the blades might be set to the wrong height for his treasured grass.

Early in our married life, I discovered that my toolbox had been removed from the cupboard and placed on a table near the window. In itself, that did no harm to anyone and his explanation was that the box was just the right height for lifting a tray of seedlings into reach of the sun's life-giving warmth. Unfortunately, seedlings need water as well as light, and I found my tools swimming in half an inch of water that had seeped into the box.

Perhaps his attitude to inanimate objects springs from a long career in the Army, where equipment belongs to a faceless employer rather than being paid for out of the soldiers' own pockets. Had I not shrieked in protest he would once have hammered in a nail with the nearest solid object to hand, a heavy glass ashtray (it happened to be a gift from a long-ago boyfriend but that I chose not to mention).

When the cast-iron plug in the lid of our solid-fuel Aga stove broke, my husband destroyed a couple of screwdrivers and several pearl-handled fish knives attempting to lever it out. Fish knives, with their thin blades, seemed to him the ideal tool. And so it proved. Unwilling to let the stove go out, he then covered the hole left by the broken plug with an antique iron we used as a doorstop. I congratulated him on his brilliant improvisation.

Despite his creative approach, I follow Mum's example. My secret stash of tools is MINE.

BREATHE IN, BREATHE OUT, SURVIVE

Ryan Prieto

My family has a cabin in the mountains near Ruidoso, New Mexico. The front porch is the perfect spot for full moon gazing on clear, cold winter nights. I'm a yoga instructor and have used Nadi Shodan, an ancient Hindu breathing practice, to keep warm while lingering in the glowing moonlight. This alternate breathing technique can calm the mind, balance the body and clear energy lines. It can even be used to raise or lower body temperature.

I sit relaxed with my spine erect and shoulders relaxed, and close my eyes. I place my left hand face up on top of my left knee and let my thumb and pointer finger touch. Then I put the tip of the index finger and middle finger of the right hand between my eyebrows, the ring finger and little finger on my left nostril and the thumb on the right nostril. I use the ring finger and little finger to open or close the left nostril and the thumb for the right nostril. Then I breathe in from the left nostril and press it closed with the ring finger and little finger. I remove the thumb from the right nostril and breathe out. Then I reverse the process, inhaling and exhaling from alternate nostrils. After ten rounds of Nadi Shodan, my body feels comfortably warm.

Nadi Shodan is a survival tool. It could save your life, if you are stranded in sub-zero weather. It can keep you cool in the desert, too. You can be your own air conditioner!

OF ALL THE TOOLBOXES IN ALL THE TOWNS IN ALL OF THE WORLD, SHE WALKS INTO MINE (WITH APOLOGIES TO RICK IN *CASABLANCA*)

Ellen E. Hyatt

When Matthew entered his home after a hard day of labor at Kennywood, the internationally-known amusement park in Pittsburgh, Pennsylvania, he was astonished to see the floor of his house. Lined from corner-to-corner of the living room were tools from his toolbox. Some of the tools he had received as gifts for accomplishment and some he had purchased after saving up wages.

There were drills, bits, hammers, and nail pullers, including the cat's paw. There were chisels, a chalk line clamp, and framer square. Even the wipedown knives were out of their proper place in the box.

He followed the carpenter's adage, "A failure to plan is a plan for failure." And he was certain he had not planned for this. It did not take him long to realize that his wife, my daughter-in-law, was at work again on a home-improvement project. Obviously, he had once again not been fast enough for the "honey-do" tasks, so Heidi had begun it herself.

Though Matthew was trained as a Master Carpenter, beginning with the Apprenticeship through Journeyman, Heidi was the master of cogent persuasion. In this case, he did not know what he was about to be coaxed into. He heard pounding coming from the kitchen.

Walking toward the sound, he saw his wife of a few sweet months hard at work on the floor. She was carefully lifting tile from the starter house they had recently purchased. To his dismay, disappointment, disgust, distress, he saw that she was pounding with a hammer into the tile with one of his prize tools: the finishing tool for drywall.

To her the tool made the perfect wedge for getting under the tile and dislodging it.

Anyone hearing the story over the years remarks how remarkable it was that the marriage had survived such house projects. To many men, messing with and misuse of prized tools would be grounds for divorce.

Cleverly, sometimes tearfully yet without tyranny, Heidi has taught Matthew that projects need to be started in a timely fashion. If not, she is likely to begin them by using the jeweled toolbox items in her own fashion.

CONDO OF FAILING APPLIANCES
OR
HAPPILY EVER AFTER INTO THE
SETTING SUN
K. Heidi Fishman

Dave and I met in early May through an internet dating service. We exchanged a few e-mails, talked on the phone (for hours) and had a first date within a few weeks. By the beginning of June we were both "hooked." We decided to take a week-long vacation to Storyland and the White Mountains with our kids — two of his and two of mine. We both wanted the kids to get to know each other and see how we all got along.

Since we had done so well finding each other on-line, we figured it wouldn't be hard to find a place to stay for our vacation week. Cyberrentals.com and an hour or so of checking out different places, we found a nice condo a stone's throw away from Storyland. It promised four bedrooms that could sleep ten, a full kitchen, and a pool in the common area building — perfect!

When we arrived at our little condo, we found the key under the fourth rock from the front door, just like the owner said we would, and let ourselves in. The place was clean and cute, but it didn't have four bedrooms, and it wasn't exactly what we had planned on. The small bedroom that we thought our girls (ages five and nine) were to share had an open electrical panel above the bed and no door to the room. That wouldn't work. The room that was supposed to have two bunk beds only had one. We dragged the mattresses from the girls "room" to the bunk room and settled all four children in there. They were certainly going to have a chance to get to know each other.

Then we sussed out the adult sleeping arrangements. We wanted to have separate sleeping quarters for us as well, to set a good example for our impressionable youngsters, but there was only one other bedroom with one bed. The couch was too short for anyone to get any sleep. We would have to make do with what was available.

The week was wonderful — hiking, the amusement park, swimming and general hanging out together. The condo on the other hand was, well, less than wonderful. Besides there not being the number of beds promised, the kitchen was strangely stocked. There were shot glasses, beer glasses, wine glasses, champagne glasses, glasses of every shape and size. However, there was only one cooking pot and there wasn't a cereal bowl to be found.

The kids enjoyed eating their Honey Nut Cheerios from margarita glasses. The toaster must have been on steroids because it flung burnt English muffins halfway across the kitchen. The dishwasher didn't work at all. We rented a video for the kids one afternoon, but the VCR ate the movie. We had to pay the video store for wrecking the tape.

I tried doing a load of laundry. The washer was great, but the dryer was dead — no heat, no power, nada, nothing. I had to hang our clothes from every conceivable piece of furniture so it all could dry. We didn't try to fix anything, we just laughed and wondered what was next.

On our fourth night we cooked dinner together. The kids were happy despite the condo's failing appliances, and after dinner while they watched TV, Dave and I stood side-by-side doing the dishes while sharing flirty whispers. He washed and I dried. As he was washing I looked down and couldn't believe what I saw — water was pouring, I mean really pouring out of the cabinet under the sink. He turned off the water and we looked inside the cabinet. The problem wasn't hard to spot. The pipe from the drain to the trap was completely disconnected. All the dirty dishwater was just going into the cabinet.

We went downstairs to look if anything had leaked down to the lower floor and the kids' room had turned into a pond. The twenty or so stuffed animals they had brought were valiantly trying to keep their heads above water. The mattresses we put on the floor were soaked. This was the great White Mountains flood of 2004.

Dave and I looked at each other. Could we fix this? Despite the fact that everyone had been having fun; despite the fact that we had paid for two more nights; despite the fact that it was a two-hour drive home and it as 8pm and we had four children under the age of ten; we both said, "Let's go home."

It took us only thirty minutes to pack our stuff, vacuum what we could and hang up all the wet bedding over doors and shower rods. We called the owner of the unit, told her we were leaving early and why, and clambered into my minivan to head west.

It was during this cleaning up and packing up that I knew I wanted to marry Dave. We were perfectly matched. We both had hit the breaking point at the same moment and knew what to do. It wasn't worth looking for duct tape or calling a plumber. We worked as a team getting out of there and keeping the kids happy. It was as if we could read each others' minds.

This was June twenty-something, one of the longest days of the year. We were headed home, with the kids happily singing songs in the back. We were winding up Route 302 into Crawford Notch, passing all the hiking spots and tourist areas that we had come to see. I was lost in my thoughts of how much I loved Dave. I couldn't say it out loud — not yet. We had only known each other for six weeks. You can't know someone well enough in six weeks to know you want to spend the rest of your life with him. And then, just as we came up over the rise of the notch, as we crested the hill between the steep rocky ledges, we were surprised by the most beautiful sunset ever. The black rocks framed the most intense color I had ever seen. It was like coming through Scylla and Charybdis. I was past the bad marriage, the divorce, the loneliness. The sky was ablaze. I can't remember the color — only the brightness, the depth and all of our reactions. All six of us were in awe. This was my burning bush, my message from the heavens. Yes, I could know someone well enough in six weeks to know I wanted to spend the rest of my life with him. I was going to marry Dave. I knew it.

If I could bottle a memory in my life, this would be it. I would return to that sunset and that realization every day. I have been married to Dave for eleven years now and I have never fallen out of love with him, but the intensity of that moment was beyond anything I had ever experienced before or since.

PRAY FOR MY HANDS
Boaz Opio

My hands need prayers. A serious prayer
They touch everything they want, they massage
different things
And later their hasty moves teach me difficult lessons
And teach me the hard things
Because they feel different things
Wrong things and right things
Every day they shake wrong hands and right hands
Yet can never accept left hands… always shaking the
right hands of men
From hotel conferences to derelicts
And everything else in between
And in the bedroom
Every time touching something as though they'd never
been touched
Both good things and bad things
Be they clean or dirty…not fearing foul

My hands need prayers…
Because they hit quickly being moved
And yet they're so quick in writing apology letters
whenever busted in quack work,
they being quick many times quake in panic
Signing up for newsletters…and later signing out
The boss says: you look idle
Then they start fidgeting with nothing immediately
Only to hand in the files and receive a cheque
And never settled for handouts from friends

My hands need prayers…
Because they all prolong from one broad chest,
a pair of muscular shoulders
Both with the same strapping physiognomy.
But one of them weaker than the other,
Yet complement one another in work,
typing as though conjoined twins of America
I ask why one then does have an upper hand over the
other?
Sidelining the brother
Neither teaching him what they know
Nor training him how to be as strong as he is

A WOMAN'S BEST FRIEND
Galia Perez

Coming from a Mexican family, I have grown up used to seeing my *Tios* use unusual tools to fix tough circumstances — like the miracles scotch tape would work when the plumber was not around to fix the leak, and when our windy El Paso weather would try to push dirt and dust through the windows. I have seen so many tools be used in so many ways, and often times our best tool was our hands, especially when we needed to give the TV a couple of hits so the antenna could kick in properly. But one day I realized I had a tool I was not aware of.

My sister and I had just moved in together making it a household of us two, her son and my two furry daughters. I knew she liked borrowing a garment here and there from previous times she would ask to borrow clothes, but I never noticed how fond she was of my closet until we started living together. I would notice my favorite shirt, shoes, jacket, pants, and scarf missing to name a few items. Being the control freak that I am, this drove me crazy. I seriously contemplated hiding a camera inside my closet to keep track of the theft or simply locking the door. But I knew neither of those options would be enough to keep my sister's sneaky hands out of there.

Apparently I wasn't the only one who found this new living situation a bit unsettling. Both of my cats let me know their displeasure when they politely marked their territory all over my room. I quickly noticed this, apologized to them and spent a whole day washing sheets, blankets and rugs to get rid of their lovely smell. Little did I know I had not cleaned their markings thoroughly, and it became evident when my sister mentioned to me that my clothes smelled a little funny and maybe I should change my detergent... How dare I?! The audacity in me to use a stinky detergent when she needs to use my clothes. Am I a bad person for finding pleasure in knowing she flaunted my Purrberry fragrance at work that day rather than my usual Chanel?

* * * * * * *

I was not sure if I was more upset at the stench my cats had left behind or my sister using my closet as her own, but soon I knew whom I would forgive. One day, after some time of me not missing any clothing items, my sister confessed the reason why she had stopped borrowing clothes. As the story went, my cats did not like her and she was surprised. My daughters learned to find refuge in the cozy, dark corners of my closet. When they would see a stranger walking in, a couple of hisses would be heard. This initially startled my darling sister but she thought that would be all they would do. What she was not expecting was, when they would see that stranger's hand rummaging through my clothes, SCRATCH! There went her hand, and if they happened to be at a lower angle and they saw feet that did not belong to their mom... SCRATCH! There went a pretty scar on her ankle. The burglar fled the scene and peace was restored into my closet.

Now don't get me wrong, I love my sister to pieces, but a woman's closet is a sensitive spot. I considered this newly received information as my cats' way of letting me know they would be my low budget security system. No fancy scotch tape or tools needed, just a woman's best friend.

WE
Jeanie Greensfelder

The sun sears hot this morning,
comes down hard.

At breakfast, we stop to laugh.
He laughs when I say
we need to get the ladder
to change a light bulb
when I mean he needs to.

We laugh extra as we age,
look at each other a second too long,
see our inner roulette wheels spin,
and know the one left standing
will remember this moment.

The sun sears hot this morning,
comes down hard.

(from Marriage and Other Leaps of Faith, Penciled In, 2015)

GOD'S GRAFFITI
J Forrest Wellman

Being born and raised in rural West Virginia might seem like a disadvantage to some people, but where else could my youth have been traumatized by stories about Bloody Bones, The Jabo, and the Barbwire Monster. Stories my New-Jersey-born-and-raised wife has banned me from telling our two young daughters. Promising me a far worse fate than anything that ever happened in one of my scary stories. But luckily, I had a true story I could tell them that topped all my spooky tales.

When I tell the story of when I had the opportunity to meet Jesus, most people roll their eyes in disbelief. I know it is hard to imagine Jesus showing up in the mountain state, even though our state slogan is "Almost Heaven."

It was late July and the dog days of summer were in full swing. My best friend Dave and I were typical sixteen year olds. We loved two things — talking to girls and fishing. I must say we were a lot better at fishing.

We had just gotten to Dave's house when his mother Dora Mae ran onto the porch, threw her hands in the air, and yelled "Halleluiah!" She then looked at us and said, "Jesus is coming today boys."

Dave curiously looked at his mother and asked what she was talking about.

His mother with tears of absolute joy in her eyes replied, "Jesus is going to appear over at the old Holden high school this evening. I just got off the phone with Lucinda and she said she had heard it from a reliable source who talked to someone who saw him there last night. So get ready, we are going to meet Jesus."

Lucinda was Dave's aunt and his mother's twin sister. After Dave's mom went back in the house, he asked me if I would go with him, and I agreed to go. How could I turn down an opportunity of such magnitude?

Dave told me not to believe everything his mother or his aunt said. He said they both were a little quirky, to put it nicely. He also told me Aunt Lucinda claimed she had recently spoken to the ghost she had seen in her house. I didn't really believe in ghosts because my father always told me, "The bad can't come back and the good don't want to." But if I had ever seen one in my house, I can assure you I wouldn't stay around long enough to talk to it.

Even though the sisters had a slight credibility problem I did know they attended church regularly. They didn't belong to any particular church. They went to all of them, including tent revivals with faith healers.

I lived just up the road, and I told Dave to stop and get me when they were ready to leave. Needless to say, I ran home to inform my parents of the spectacular news. My mom was gone, so I told my dad what I had heard. To my surprise he didn't seem to be impressed.

He calmly replied, "If Jesus is there, you come back and let me know so I can bring the rest of the family to see him."

It wasn't long till Dave and his mom pulled in the driveway and blew the car horn. I hurried out the door and got in the car, because it was July hot and no one wants to be kept waiting in a hot car.

We had no more than pulled out when Dora Mae informed us she was stopping to pick up her sister Lucinda to go with us. When we pulled up in front of her house, Lucinda came out and had her daughter Cecilia with her. They were dressed in church clothes, and Lucinda was carrying her Bible. She got in the front and Cecilia got in the back seat with Dave and me. I had a crush on Cecilia for a long time and was more than happy to sit beside her.

We were off, and hadn't gone far when we stopped again to pick up Jenny, a friend of Lucinda's. Jenny also was dressed for church and got in the front seat. Now there were six of us crammed in this car with no air conditioning.

We were almost to the old school when Dave asked his Aunt Lucinda if she was going to get Jesus to autograph her Bible.

Lucinda got mad and yelled, "No I don't want him to autograph my bible! I will get to hear all I need to hear straight from Him. I don't even need this Bible now that he is back."

She then threw the bible at Dave. He ducked and it landed in the rear window next to the bobble head dog.

She then started singing the hymn Just A Little Talk With Jesus. Dora Mae and Jenny quickly joined in, and the three of them sang hymns the remainder of the trip.

We finally made it to the old school, and I was amazed that there were so many people there. There had to be at least fifty people standing around. I started to think these women might be right and that Jesus was going to appear. I mean, all these people seem to believe it. Dora Mae and Lucinda along with Jenny quickly disappeared into the crowd. Dave, Cecilia and I stayed close to the car and watched the crowd from a distance. It kept growing as it got darker.

My curiosity got the better of me so I made my way over to the crowd. At that moment the streetlights came on and I heard someone yell, "THERE HE IS!" I looked in the direction from where the yell came and could see nothing. Then another person yelled, "I see him!" Then another. Everyone close to the old school house appeared to be seeing Him, so the rest of the people started pushing to get closer.

The crowd was getting loud with words of praise and hollering, "Halleluiah!" Then I could hear a man with a high-pitched voice preaching. Was this the voice of Jesus, I wondered.

I squeezed my way to the front of the crowd. There he was, right in front of me. He didn't look like the pictures we have all seen hanging in our homes and churches. He didn't have long hair or wear a robe or sandals. This man had a flat-top haircut and was on the chubby side. He wore blue jeans, a t-shirt and a pair of white Converse All Stars. His hell fire and brimstone sermon had the crowd riled up and they answered, "Amen!" to just about every word that came out of his mouth. After listening to him preach for a few minutes I realized his accent sounded local and he kept saying, "Praise be to Jesus." I concluded this man was not Jesus. I knew we had been duped.

I turned to walk away when a lady said, "Did you see him?"

"No," I replied.

She answered back, "I had trouble at first, too, but now I can." She pointed to the large tree behind the man preaching. I looked and behold I could see him clearly. Not the real Jesus but the image of him in the outline of the tree. The streetlight behind the tree gave it a kind of halo effect. A smile came on my face as I stood there and looked. I wondered how this tree came to be this way and if it was some kind of sign of something to come. After I thought about it for a few minutes, I concluded only God could have created such a wondrous sight.

I then walked back to the car and told Dave and Cecilia that it was a tree that looked like Jesus. To my surprise they didn't laugh or make any jokes. They went and saw it, and agreed it looked amazing.

Later we started on our journey home, and Lucinda and Dora Mae laughed about their being misinformed but agreed it was worth the trip. Lucinda got her Bible out of the back window of the car and apologized to Dave for throwing it at him.

It is memories like this that I treasure the most from growing up in the mountain state. I have seen other things like the Jesus tree that looked as if Mother Nature had some help. Like a thirty-foot tall boulder shaped just like a boot. There is also Waffle rock. I challenge anyone to look at it and tell me how else it could have been made without some help from the Big Man. The list goes on and so does my never-ending search for what I have come to call God's Graffiti. All a person has to do is open their eyes when they are in this wild and truly wonderful West Virginia. The place I have always been proud to call my home.

Footnote: Online you can find photos and newspaper articles about the "Jesus Tree" located in Logan, West Virginia. Boot Rock is located in Williamson, West Virginia, north of the field house. Waffle Rock is a rock formation in Mineral County, West Virginia.

KIDS GET THE CRAZIEST IDEAS. . .
Phylis Warady

The prime lesson learned from my kids is that parenthood is an iffy journey in which one's parenting skills are constantly tested. My ongoing trial began mere hours after carting home from the hospital my firstborn and continued on for the next twenty or so years. With yours truly cast in the role of a woefully sleep-deprived parent. Especially true once hubby, though initially eager to share the burden, felt obliged to take a second job – that of a cab driver – thus unavailable to pitch in from supper time to daybreak

Shaken by the loss of my helpmate in the wee hours, I was all too often faced with nightly stints of pacing the floor with a colicky babe, or a bit later on, one cutting her first tooth. Panicked by her pitiful wails, I turned for advice to my BFF. The seasoned mother of twin toddlers, she kindly reminded me of the teething ring she'd gifted me with shortly after my daughter's birth. She also recommended first rubbing my daughter's raw gums with brandy before insertion of the teething ring.

I didn't have any brandy on hand. So I decided to substitute cognac. Mere seconds after insertion of the ring, my daughter's tiny hand latched onto it. Then silence reigned. Feeling blessed, I decided to celebrate my reprieve by treating myself to a healthy swig of hubby's aged Hennessy.

Moreover, despite all those early trials I faced alone, there were lighter moments to treasure. Consequently, I am now willing share this um...gem with other formerly beleaguered parents, now bent upon spoiling their grandkids.

Shortly after Anne Christine turned five, she observed, "Mommy, our family has two girls and only one boy. We need a baby brother."

Since April Carolyn was just two and Stephen MacDougal barely one, her suggestion unsettled me. Nevertheless, I roused myself to ask, "If we did have another boy, what would we call him?"

Anne promptly replied, "George MacHanical."

George MacHanical? No way. Though proud of my smidgen of Scottish blood, one must know when to draw the line.

Three years passed before Stephen, now four, demanded a brother to play with. Rattled, I swiftly changed the subject.

A week later, he cornered me to demand, "Where is he?"

Drawing a deep fortifying breath, I said babies are sweet but take a lot of work. Then added, "Each day I swallow a pill that prevents me from having any more kids."

Stephen's eyes lost their sparkle. But minutes later, he rallied. "When we were babies, did Daddy help?"

"Did he ever!" I enthused. "For several months, not only did he take care of most of the two o'clock feedings, he changed your wet diapers."

After mulling this over, Stephen said, "Mom, you've got nothing to worry about. Just quit taking those pills, and Daddy and I will take care of everything."

George MacHanical? To tell the truth, I never found the courage.

In conclusion, while parenting is an onerous challenge designed to test one's mettle and, at times, one's sanity, the end result is well worth each gray hair justly earned.

PEAK EXPERIENCES
Jeanie Greensfelder

Hopeful, I accept a party invitation.
A valet takes my car. The hosts and their dog
greet me. I meet Oopsi, a tall poodle, named
for accidents caused by her wagging tail.

A white-jacketed waiter offers me a martini,
stokes me for the buzzing clusters of people
trying to connect over movies, books, and trips,
hoping, like me, to be seen and heard. I carry
a security blanket, a topic to discuss: Maslow's
moments of high happiness called peak experiences.

I'm relieved when Trudy appears with her
waterfall of words: A bead fell off my gown
and the seamstress fixing it had a heart attack. I called
a locksmith and broke in to retrieve this dress
for tonight. She shows where the bead is missing.
In my plain black knit, ready to move on, I say,

Excuse me, I need to say hello to someone.
Like glue, Trudy says, I'll come with you.

Oopsi rubs her white curls on tuxedoed legs. She smells
bacon-wrapped appetizers. Her nose quivers.
Trudy and I want treats too. We follow Oopsi
to a group being served. Patrice complains,
the food's fatty, grabs another, and says, I have reflux.

Migraines, backaches, kidney stones, prostates,
and menopause symptoms compete, ending with Trudy's
I almost died and Patrice's I wanted to kill myself.

When I suggest talking about peak experiences,
Trudy drones on about Aspen; Patrice, about the Alps.

I move away, fill a plate at the buffet, and sit by Oopsi.
She looks into my eyes and listens to everything I say.

I'M TAKING FISH STICKS OUT OF THE FREEZER

Sarah Dickenson Snyder

"How many do you want, Abby?"
"Five," her head down near the "V" of her book.
"How about you, David?"

"Six," he says looking up from Calvin and Hobbes.
"Did you say 'sex'?" Abby asks, eyes widened.
"No," he says quietly. Okay here we go –

moving without a clear plan
but a vague one – answer honestly,
don't overwhelm. I ask her,

"What do you know about 'sex'?"
"Allie told me about it last night at the sleep over."
"What did she say?" David asks and I think.

"Sex is when two people are naked in bed."
I slide the pan in the oven, close the door,
"That's true," I say. Some silence, then she asks,

"Have you done sex, Mom?"
"Yes, I have," I say. More silence.
"Why?" she asks.

"Why?" I repeat. Stalling, of course – because
it feels so perfect, because I disappear…
"Well, sex is how babies get made."

Everyone seems satisfied, perhaps an ending, but no,
David is calculating as usual, eager to be right,
"You've done it twice!"

True-ish. "Yes, yeah I have,"
I say. We're good, we can move on –
everyone feeling fine. "Can two boys do sex?

or two girls?" David asks.
"Yes they can, but they won't
make babies," I say.

"I'm hungry," Abby says.
We're good? We're done?
"Me, too," David says.

IS NOT A CANDLE ALWAYS A TOOL OF INSPIRATION?

Denise "Deni" Gainer

Once upon a time — all good stories start that way, don't they?

Way back in the mid 1980's, I worked in the largest locker room in the county. That would be for a law enforcement agency, which shall remain unnamed for everyone's protection! I was hired because I was a reporter with excellent reputation and that is what this new sheriff wanted reflected in his Public Information staff.

So, I became a PIO, Public Information Officer. I became a middle-man between investigating officers and the news media, dispensing crime scene information. That later included writing and publishing two agency newsletters, one for deputies and staff, and one for the public. Later, that also included learning law enforcement policy and procedure and writing the agency manual, and eventually becoming a certified law enforcement trainer.

These duties, all while I was a civilian — meaning, I was sworn-at as opposed to sworn-in. Almost needless to say, I had to become very creative in dealing with these law enforcement types in order to get them to do what I needed them to do in order for them to stay certified and keep doing their job.

That was no easy task, as I was female, civilian, and a former reporter — an enemy on all fronts! So, I had to prove myself every step of the way. First, it was working out in the gym. So, you could say, it was gym equipment I first used, untraditionally, as a tool to build trust and relationships. Soon, the LEOS, Law Enforcement Officers, could see I was functioning and meeting their required levels of physical fitness.

Then, as officers brought me projects they needed to have done, I used words and art to convey their thoughts as my next tools from my box. LEO lingo is very rigid and not open to creative interpretation. Once they could see that my translation to the public made them look good and respectable, then my professional life and theirs got easier.

The next role I would assume would prove more challenging. I don't care if you are the Sheriff himself/herself, deputies DO NOT like to come to a classroom to learn something! And if you are a civilian, certified LEO trainer or not, "What on God's Green Earth can we possibly learn from you?" is their attitude.

Male or female, those deputies were armed, literally and mentally, against me. So…how to get them to drop their weapons and actually enjoy their mandatory education became my focus. First, rewriting lesson plans became a must. They were all lecture style. Blah!

Everyone hates that! So using my words again, I made everything as interactive as I could to keep students engaged and possibly have fun as they learned exciting things like *Report Writing, Bloodborne Pathogens, TeamBuilding, Record Keeping,* and *Cultural Diversity.*

Next, I had to look at my wardrobe. Yes, clothes became a tool. My audience was 98% men. (Always know your audience!) So, dressing professionally but appealingly was next step. Always a nice crisp white cotton button shirt, that was perhaps left unbuttoned one button a little lower than might be expected.

That tool was employed because, and it was ALWAYS predictable, deputies fill up the back of the room first (because they don't want to be there and the situation is an unknown — they are trained to be cautious). Well, I needed them up front because I was not going to yell or otherwise use up all my energy moving from back to front in the classroom!

Invariably, I would have to approach the squad lieutenant, slightly bend over to his desk-sitting level and explain that as his being leader of the group, it would be a marvelous example if he led his squad to the front of the room to show enthusiasm for learning what they needed to keep their certification. And, of course, words were always chosen to make him feel special.

So, tools used — clothes and words.

Next, how to keep their attention on most topics that just are boring as H-E-Double-Hockey Sticks!

As it happened to be, for my hobby amusement, I sold candles and taught aromatherapy at that time, too. It dawned on me that using the largest pillar candle I could find would be the perfect conversation piece!

So, after roll-call and my stating the goal of the class at hand, I would offer one other instruction before I began teaching. I would present a 12-inch pointed (or bell-top) vanilla candle to the students, with the directive that it be handled by each student, sniffed for as long as seemed appropriate, and then passed on continually throughout the class. The candle was to stay moving from student to student for the entire class.

Well, the sarcasm and laughter immediately surfaced. "What are we doing THAT for?!?" (If you understand locker room mentality, then you can image all the sex comments that the deputies offered.) And my response was always, "Just keep it going and after your test, at close of the class, I'll happily tell you why."

And so, now with open and curious minds, I began to pour the information they needed into their otherwise *I-know-it-all* brains.

Most classes were half-day. Others were 40-hours. No matter the topic or length of the class, with appropriate breaks and class exercises, the vanilla candle kept going. At the end of each class, after the exam, which all consistently passed with flying-colors, I would always be asked "why" the candle was passed.

And, always, the candle would somehow disappear. So, I would say, "When the magic candle reappears on the desk behind me, I will *for sure* tell you why we kept sniffing and passing the candle." Then I would turn and erase the dry-erase board and miraculously, the candle would appear.

And so it was, I would sigh with glee explaining that all had passed with scores well-above norm and that was due, in part, to the vanilla candle. They would laugh, sarcasm in full display.

Then I would ask if anyone had ever heard of aromatherapy. Trust me. None of them ever had. So, I would explain that the fragrances stimulate the mind and certain fragrances "do" certain things! And, the lovely smell of vanilla triggers an "opening of the mind"! My closing line — "*Obviously*, it worked for you *all!!!* Thank you and enjoy the rest of your day!" To which, there was applause, chatter and laughter.

Mission Accomplished. Next class, all filled the room from the front back, and another, different, fragrant candle would be passed.

ABOUT THE AUTHORS

Patty Crocker, M.D., practiced emergency medicine in El Paso, Texas, and rural New Mexico for twenty years. In 2011, she became interested in the new medical specialty of anti-aging. Dr. Crocker is board certified in anti-aging and rejuvenative medicine. In 2013, she founded the Del Norte Wellness Center in El Paso, Texas, where she practices today.

Katie Eber holds a B.A. in English Literature from Roanoke College (Class of '11) and is a 2014 graduate from the Master of Fine Arts in Creative Writing program at Fairfield University. Katie's work has appeared in *On Concept's Edge, Hobo Pancakes, Garbanzo Literary Journal, Quail Bell Magazine,* and *MadHad Lit.*

K. Heidi Fishman is a psychologist by training, but more importantly, she is an observer and writer of the human condition. You can find her blog at PopjeAndMe. com. A member of the League of Vermont Writers, she lives in Norwich, Vermont, with her husband, children and a feisty border terrier.

Richard R. Ford is Professor Emeritus of Languages and Linguistics at the University of Texas at El Paso, having taught and published numerous studies in the field of Spanish<—>English translation and Spanish American literature. In retirement, he plays poker, sips chardonnay and writes poetry, essays and short narrative fiction in English.

Denise "Deni" Gainer is a published writer of more than forty years! At least, that's all the number of trips around the Sun she is claiming as a professional. A Floridian since college days, she is now semi-retired. An avid gardener, she still teaches peaceful things like Meditation, Candle Magic, and other Mother Nature stuff. "Once a writer, always a writer. Hope you enjoy my tool tale!"

Dana Glossbrenner is a retired English teacher and school counselor. She has lived in West Texas most of her life and has written dozens of short stories set in that area. She also has published a nonfiction book, *Women Behind Stained Glass: West Texas Pioneers*, and is in the process of publishing her first novel, *Skylark Spring*.

Ibeji Grace was born in Abia state, Nigeria. She obtained her primary education in Umuahia and had her secondary school education at Holy Rosary Girls College in Umuahia. She is currently a Jambite. Although she is a science student, she loves reading and writing. She has also written many unpublished stories.

Carol Graham, author, motivational speaker, radio show host and health coach, shares the art of becoming a survivor based on her own traumatic life experiences.

In her weekly blog and radio show, Carol shares inspirational, motivational and heart-warming stories of people who have overcome insurmountable odds and became successful. She is a regular contributor to several websites and has been published in three anthologies.

Jeanie Greensfelder is the author of *Marriage and Other Leaps of Faith* and *Biting the Apple*. Her poems can be found on *Writer's Almanac*, the *Poetry Foundation*, jeaniegreensfelder.com, in journals and online under her name.

A psychologist, she seeks to understand herself and others on this shared journey, filled, as Joseph Campbell wrote, with sorrowful joys and joyful sorrows.

Petei Guth is a multi-talented artist specializing in the Big Bend area. She has been a Tierra Grande Texas Master Naturalist in Alpine, Texas, for over eleven years.

Her jewelry, drawings, note cards and photography are her main focus. For over thirty five years she was a nationally known needlepoint artist and designer, and studied at the Dallas Art Institute in Dallas, Texas.

Fellow of the Western Pennsylvania Writing Project, professor, columnist, and appointee to the Board of Governors of the South Carolina Academy of Authors, **Ellen E. Hyatt** serves organizations promoting literacy and the arts. She resides in Summerville, South Carolina, with her husband David and does not lay hands on any toolboxes.

Barbara Kirchner, artist and writer, resides in Jarrettsville, Maryland. Her professional career includes Life Membership in the National League of American Pen Women (Art and Letters), the Baltimore Watercolor Society, and Maryland Pastel Society, among others. Poetry and informative articles have appeared in *Towne & Country Life Magazine, Chesapeake Literary Review, Gunpowder Review, Liriodendron Review,* and P*en Woman Magazine.*

Mark Knobloch was born and raised in Baltimore, Maryland. After graduating from Washington and Lee University, Mark returned to Baltimore to begin his career in commercial real estate. He also earned a Master of Science degree in Real Estate from Johns

Hopkins University. Mark is married to Denise and has two college-aged daughters, Baylor and Campbell.

Margaret Hunter Malpass and her husband, Mitch, live on the Hunter Family Farm, where she grew up. They returned there thirty-seven years ago and renovated a pre-Civil War house. Their home is located two miles north of Turkey, North Carolina, in Sampson County. Sampson is the largest swine producing county in North Carolina, which is second only to Iowa in production.

Madeleine McDonald lives on the chilly east coast of England where the wind whistles up through the floorboards. She writes light-hearted newspaper columns on family life, poetry and short stories. Her third romance novel, *A Shackled Inheritance*, was published in 2016.

mariana mcdonald's work has appeared in numerous publications, including poetry in *Crab Orchard Review, Lunch Ticket*, and *Stone Sea and Sky. An Anthology of Georgia Poems,* and fiction in *So to Speak, UpDo and Cobalt*, where she was a finalist for the Zora Neale Hurston Fiction Prize. She became a Fellow of Georgia's Hambidge Arts Center in 2012.

Carole Ann Moleti lives and works in New York City and writes fiction and nonfiction that focuses on women's and political issues. Her work ranges from sweet and sentimental in the *Shifts and This Path* anthologies to edgy and irreverent in the *Not Your Mother's Book Series*. She was the winner of Oasis Journal's 2009 prize for creative nonfiction.

Ben Musick (1905-1975) was the father of **Jack L. Musick and Kathleen Musick Beeby Gancer**. Jack attended Oklahoma State University and farmed in Kingfisher, Oklahoma, until he retired. He has four children and seven grandchildren.

His sister, Kathleen Musick Gancer, graduated from Oklahoma State University and has three children and seven grandchildren. She moved to North Carolina in 1989 where she and her husband have retired. They grew up in a farming family who also owned a gasoline/service station and lumber company.

Born in 1990 to a poor village in the Eastern Uganda district of Tororo, **Boaz Opio** attended primary school and secondary education between 1997 and 2008 before travelling westwards to the capital of Kampala to find work.

The city of Kampala is a great place for nurturing solitude and critical philosophy where Boaz now lives the life of a writer living alone in a cottage.

Carl "Papa" Palmer of Old Mill Road in Ridgeway, Virginia, now lives in University Place, Washington. He has a 2015 contest winning poem riding buses somewhere in Seattle. Carl is a Pushcart Prize and Micro Award nominee. MOTTO: Long Weekends Forever www.authorsden.com/carlpalmer

Galia Perez is a graduate of the University of Texas in El Paso, and is as hairstylist. She lives in El Paso with her son, Ari, who is watched over by her cats.

Ryan Prieto is a graduate of New Mexico State University. She is founder and owner of Casa de Yoga in El Paso, Texas. She is a certified Reiki practitioner and is certified in Thai yoga therapy.

JoAnna Scandiffio is a poet, educator and gemologist living in San Francisco. Her poems capture the oddness of the everyday, the out-of-place. She is always looking for the catch of the day. Her poems have appeared in *Sugared Water, Switched-on Gutenberg, Naugatuck River Review* and *ellipsis…literature & art.*

Sarah Dickenson Snyder has been writing poetry since she knew there was a form with conscious line breaks. Pertinent to her work as a writer, she has been an English teacher for many years, a mother for several, and student and participant in poetry workshops, classes, and writing conferences. Sarah was lucky to be a part of the Bread Loaf Writers' Conference and to have several poems published in magazines, journals, and book anthologies.

Tony Stafford was born in Belmont, North Carolina. He received a BA from Wake Forest University, an MA from the University of Texas at El Paso, and a PhD in English from Louisiana State University. He has published numerous books, scholarly articles on Shakespeare, Renaissance Poems, and modern British and American playwrights such as Shaw and Mamet. He has also written numerous plays produced from Los Angeles to Denver, Houston to Washington, D.C.

Lisa Timpf is a freelance writer who lives in Simcoe, Ontario, Canada. Her writing has been published in a variety of venues, including *Chicken Soup for the Soul: Christmas in Canada, Good Times, Small Farm Canada, The Martian Wave, Morel Magazine,* and *New Myths.*

Phylis Warady, now age eighty six, began writing award-winning short stories, essays, memoir-vignettes and light verse when her three kids were ages five, two and one to save her sanity. To stave off hunger pangs she's also the author of six published historical novels set in Regency England (1811-20).

J Forrest Wellman is a coal miner and freelance writer, proudly born and raised in the mountains of Southern West Virginia. He loves his morning coffee, classic movies and time spent in the hills of his beloved state. He lives in Charleston, West Virginia, with his "New Jersey" wife and their two amazing young daughters.

Jen Wynkoop is a New York-based comedy writer and self-proclaimed "independent woman who don't need no man." She graduated with honors from Syracuse University in 2013 with a major in Television, Radio, and Film, and a dual-minor in English and Bro Studies. She spends her free time drinking wine, overfeeding her dog, and getting excessively worked up watching "House Hunters."

ABOUT THE EDITORS

Marta Knobloch is a poet and author. She has written four award-winning collections of poetry. Her work has appeared in numerous literary magazines and anthologies in the United States, Australia, Ireland, Italy and England. She has traveled extensively throughout her life, lived abroad, and now makes her home in Monroe, Georgia. To learn more about her work, visit www.martaknobloch.com

Kip Piper is an international best-selling Amazon author, including her *Make Money Online Entrepreneur Series* and her line of Kip aDoodles adult coloring books www.kipadoodles.com. She enjoys hiking, cooking, traveling, and spending time with friends and family. Kip has recently moved back to her hometown of Warrenton, Virgina, to be closer to her roots.

www.ingramcontent.com/pod-product-compliance
Lightning Source LLC
Chambersburg PA
CBHW071549040426
42452CB00008B/1114